LOVING GOD'S FAMILY

Roy Matheson

This book is designed for your personal reading
pleasure and profit. It is also designed for group
study. A Leader's Guide with helps and hints for
teachers is available from your local bookstore
or from the publisher.

VICTOR

BOOKS a division of SP Publications, Inc.

WHEATON, ILLINOIS 60187

Offices also in
Whitby, Ontario, Canada
Amersham-on-the-Hill, Bucks, England

All Scripture quotations are taken from the *Holy Bible: New International Version,* © 1978 by the New York International Bible Society. Used by the permission of Zondervan Bible Publishers. Other quotations are from the *New American Standard Bible,* (NASB) © the Lockman Foundation 1960, 1962, 1963, 1968, 1971, 1972, 1973, 1975, 1977.

Recommended Dewey Decimal Number: 227.94
Suggested Subject Heading: N.T.: 1 John

Library of Congress Catalog Card Number: 84-52041
ISBN: 0-89693-524-8

VICTOR BOOKS
A division of SP Publications, Inc.
Wheaton, Illinois 60187

Contents

To Helen
Who lives out the truths
in this book on a daily basis

With appreciation to Audrey Sullivan,
for her labor of love on the manuscript

1 Surveying the Landscape

Gary Kervin gunned his car out of the garage and down the driveway. He narrowly missed a telephone pole as he pulled onto the street. Driving to work, he repeatedly cut in front of other drivers; it was a miracle he wasn't involved in a serious accident. At the office, he found himself making a number of mistakes in his work. He left the office at 5:05 and drove home, a feeling of complete depression enveloping him.

Gary is not incompetent at his work. In fact, his superior recently recommended him for a promotion when a vacancy opens up. He also is a good driver. He's never been involved in an accident and hasn't received a traffic ticket in five years.

Actually, his problems started at the breakfast table that morning. He had disagreed with his wife Sarah about whether to send their ten-year-old son back to camp for the summer. Gary felt the cost was prohibitive; his wife disagreed. Their son, Joe, put in his two cents' worth and a heated argument developed. Gary

5

rose from the table, grabbed his briefcase, and stomped out the door without even saying good-bye. And therein was the source of his problems.

Basically, Gary's inability to function *outside* his family was the result of unresolved tensions *within* his family. By failing to restore and improve his family relationships, Gary remained ineffective in all that he did. He was struggling to survive.

The church also is struggling for survival today. The society of the late twentieth century seems unimpressed with the life of the average Christian; many men and women see nothing in the church they covet for themselves. Christians seem unable to reverse this trend. Why is this so?

I believe that Christians are ineffective *outside* the church because of unresolved tensions *within* the church. The body of Christ is much like the Kervin family. We will continue to be ineffective in our world unless we, as Christians, resolve our differences, alleviate our tensions, and work on quality relationships inside the family of faith. It's that simple—and that complex.

This is where 1 John can help us. It is a book, if you will, about the family. The author writes at the end of the first century to a group of Christians infected and torn apart by false teaching. These believers needed direction for the future and reassurance concerning their spiritual status in the present.

John seeks to meet their needs by helping these believers rediscover the dynamic of ministering to one another within the Christian community. He explains that when they gave their allegiance to Christ, they also joined a special family—the family of God. As such, they share God's life and have a responsibility to exhibit "family characteristics" to other family members. John works from the premise that Christians will never be effective *outside* the church until they first experience meaningful spiritual relationships *within* it.

It is in this setting that John's book has value for us. Contemporary Christianity has lost its vision of the church as a family. When we do gather as a group, we seem more like a crowd assembled to hear a lecture than a family caring for each other. Perhaps I should not be surprised by this. After all, we are rugged individualists by tradition and by temperament; we are prone to live the Christian life in isolation, responsible to no one but ourselves.

John's thrust for the first-century church fits us as well. The church cannot be effective in society unless we resolve our own inner tensions and minister meaningfully to the saints.

For 1 John to be of value to us, then, we must place ourselves in the position of its first readers. Only when we identify with their problems can we use this epistle to solve our own. Only when we attain the same understanding of God and His Word can we too become unified as His family.

Identifying the Enemy

A group of false teachers had infiltrated the early church and had left their stamp on it. John refers to these teachers as antichrists (2:18) and as possessing the spirit of error (4:3). They once had been part of the fellowship, but only in a superficial, outward sense. A crisis had developed and they departed, taking some of the church members with them. "They went out from us, but they did not really belong to us," John observes (2:19). Unfortunately, these false teachers still exerted an influence over a number of the members who stayed behind. John, therefore, is keenly interested in neutralizing the false teachers' efforts.

Establishing the identity of these teachers is somewhat difficult. Have you ever listened to one end of a two-way telephone conversation? You can hear the answers given by the person you're with, but it's a little more difficult to piece together the questions being asked at the other end of the line. In 1 John, we can hear John's response to the error being propagated, but we're not told exactly *what* false doctrines were being taught. In other words, we are not given a systematic treatment of the erroneous beliefs about which John was concerned; however, he does make several statements throughout his epistle which provide us with some strong clues.

Scholars generally agree that these false teachers were Gnostics, a sect that believed the material world was intrinsically evil. Gnostics concluded that Jesus could not be God in the flesh because He could not inhabit an evil human body. They taught that man could achieve salvation by possessing knowledge that only was available to members of their group. Since knowledge was all-important, the matter of living a holy and righteous life lost its significance. It was not *how* a person behaved, but *what* he knew that guaranteed direct access to God.

The Gnostics have long since disappeared. They pose no threat to us today. Some of their teaching, however, continues to plague us as it reappears in different forms. The church—like the Gnostics— often has viewed the material world as intrinsically evil, though God made it good (Gen. 1). We compartmentalize everything into spiritual things (good) and material things (evil). Money and possessions are seen as evil, in and of themselves, though it is the *love* of these things that Scripture condemns (1 Tim. 6:10).

The modern church also tends to view the physical bodies as evil, though the Bible tells us we are to offer our bodies for service (Rom. 12:1-2). Paul explains it well:

Do not offer the parts of your body to sin, as instruments of wickedness, but rather offer yourselves to God, as those who have returned from death to life; and offer the parts of your body to Him as instruments of righteousness (Rom. 6:13).

Like the Gnostics, the church often places knowledge above Christian experience. What really matters is how many Bible verses I can quote verbatim, and whether I can trace Paul's thought through the Book of Romans. Such displays are considered more crucial than living a life of holiness and love before my neighbors. More value is placed on memorizing eschatological charts and having all the events of Christ's return in chronological order than on living each day in eager expectancy of Christ's return.

This does not mean that knowing the Bible and its contents is unimportant. We must have a firm grasp of biblical data if we are to apply these truths to life. But there is something more important than mastering the Bible. We must allow the Bible to master us. If we do not, we will drift dangerously close to the same error that trapped some of John's readers—that of divorcing spiritual knowledge from spiritual experience and glorying in our knowledge alone.

One final item concerning these teachers is worth mentioning. The false teachers of John's day placed such a high premium on their knowledge that they saw themselves as a spiritually elite cadre. They alone had the answers. God could be known only if one was a member of their group. This same spiritual elitism is with us today. *Our* group has a corner on the truth. Only *our* church interprets the Bible correctly. Others may be Christians, but they are second-class citizens in the kingdom of God.

You may well have a significant grasp of spiritual truth. Perhaps you have been a student of the Scriptures for decades. Perhaps the pages of your Bible are worn and wrinkled from constant use. Yet John's first epistle is quick to condemn exclusivism. "You have an anointing from the Holy One, and all of you know the truth," he states (1 John 2:20). A knowledge of God is not the private property of any special interest group. There always is significant new ground to cover; we never can know it all. We would do well to remember, then, that the truth is available to Christians in ecclesiastical traditions other than our own. A recognition of this fact can help reduce tensions in God's family and increase our love for one another.

Discovering the Purpose

John writes these chapters between A.D. 90-100. Obviously, the Apostle lived in a world quite different from our own; yet the specific reasons for his penning this epistle are not irrelevant for us. Why? Because man's basic spiritual needs have not changed. The same needs John discovered in this first-century congregation are present in our lives today. Three of John's purposes for writing should, accordingly, be mentioned.

To Provide Assurance. The dogmatic claims of the false teachers made many of John's flock uneasy about their status with God. Some wondered how it was possible to know they had a personal relationship with the Father. John's words are designed to convince them it *is* possible to be certain:

- We know that we have come to know Him (2:3);
- You have known Him who is from the beginning (2:13);
- We know that we belong to the truth (3:19);
- We know that we live in Him and He in us (4:13);
- You may know that you have eternal life (5:13).

John thus writes with practical concern to his "dear children" and assures them that they *can* be sure of their relationship with God. Certainty comes not from joining an exclusive little group, but by seeing the evidence of God's life within us.

Jane talked with me one night after a youth meeting. She was nineteen and exuded a confident, vivacious personality—on the outside. Her inner life was filled with turmoil. She had made a "decision" for Christ two years earlier, but was constantly plagued by doubts. Her behavior was not consistent with her beliefs, and she was doubtful about her relationship with God. I shared these verses from 1 John with her, and they brought a measure of stability to her turbulent faith. This is a major reason God included this book in the New Testament.

To Portray the Divine-Human Christ. In our own day, people who refuse to acknowledge Christ as their Lord often do so because they cannot reconcile the divine and human aspects of His nature. It is difficult for an age cluttered with technological marvels to believe that a real person could raise the dead and walk on water.

In many ways, the New Testament world was quite different from our own. Stories of divine men who visited the earth and supposedly performed miraculous feats were easily accepted. But by the time of the first-century church, men already had difficulty believing that a miracle-working person could be a genuine human being. Thus, many did not believe Christ actually possessed an earthly body.

John responds to this disbelief by emphasizing the reality of Christ's body and His human nature. He begins his letter by insisting that he *personally* had heard, seen, looked at, and touched this Christ (1:1). Christians today may de-emphasize Christ's humanity in their hurry to prove His deity. Yet John brings the human nature of Christ into balance with His divinity.

To Produce Guidelines to Test the Reality of Our Faith. How can one test the reality of his or her spiritual beliefs? It is not enough to repeat the proper clichés and pious slogans. John provides his readers with a series of tests to measure the depth of their Christian commitment. These tests are threefold in nature: we must exercise love, practice righteousness, and demonstrate correct belief. We encounter these tests repeatedly as we move through the epistle.

John explains the components of the "love test" in the following verses: "Whoever loves his brother lives in the light" (2:10); "We know that we have passed from death to life because we love our brothers" (3:14); "Everyone who loves has been born of God and knows God" (4:7).

With respect to righteousness, we hear John saying: "You know that everyone who does what is right has been born of Him" (2:29), and "This is how we know who the children of God are and who the children of the devil are: Anyone who does not do what is right is not a child of God" (3:10).

The matter of correct personal belief is addressed through such words as, "No one who denies the Son has the Father; whoever acknowledges the Son has the Father also" (2:23), and "Everyone who believes that Jesus is the Christ is born of God" (5:1).

These three tests of true Christianity are not to be taken in isolation, but together, since each complements the other. They are to be lived simultaneously in the life of the believer.

Not long ago, I labored to repair a small toaster in our kitchen. Three isolated wires, each a different color, entered the appliance. From outside the toaster, it was easy to tell them apart. As I traced them into the narrow confines of the appliance, however, they became so intertwined it was impossible to separate them from one another. The same should be true of John's three tests. One can separate the tests at certain points in 1 John, but that is not really what the author intends for us to do. The tests are intertwined and inseparable; all three should be observable in a believer's daily experience.

Getting the Big Picture

Shortly after I moved to Toronto, I took an elevator to the top of the tallest building in the city. It was a clear day and I could make out the major arteries carrying traffic east and west, north and south. It helped me get my bearings in this metropolis and decreased the likelihood of my getting lost as I traveled through its individual neighborhoods.

In the same way, we need to get the "big picture" for this little epistle. We need to be able to follow its thoughts without getting lost in its individual chapters. In short, we need an outline for it. Unfortunately, this is not the easiest of books to map out.

For example, 1 John makes repeated use of such

phrases as: "If we claim" (1:6, 8, 10); "Anyone who claims" (2:6, 9); and "If anyone says" (4:20). In passages like these, John is quoting the statements of the false teachers and refuting them. At other times, he uses their terminology, but baptizes it with new meaning. The heretics used words such as "anointing" (2:20) and "seed" (3:9); John steals them and puts them to his own use.

It is for such reasons that 1 John is rather difficult to get a handle on. Because the Apostle is busy responding to various aspects of false doctrine, the epistle's content does not always fit into tidy little packages. Its structure has been described by some as a spiral; the author tends to take his readers in a circle, and then starts over again at the same point—but in a slightly different way. Others have suggested that the book's format mirrors a symphony. John's great themes rise to the surface, recede, and come to the foreground again in another context.

Each of these analogies possesses some merit in describing this epistle's sometimes confusing layout. Nevertheless, I believe it *is* possible to suggest a general outline for the book.

Chapter 1 begins with an emphasis on life: "This we proclaim concerning the Word of life. The life appeared. . . . We proclaim to you the eternal life" (1:1-2). The book ends on a similar note, "He is the true God and eternal life" (5:20). The intervening material in the book describes what is involved in enjoying life "in the family" and falls into three basic themes.

Living in God's Family Means Walking in the Light (1:1—2:17)

John makes several references to light in this section: "God is light" (1:5); "If we walk in the light" (1:7);

"The true light is already shining" (2:8); "Anyone who claims to be in the light" (2:9); "Whoever loves his brother lives in the light" (2:10). In essence, walking in the light means living a life consistent with the character of God.

John develops this theme in a threefold way. First, he probes the *problem* that keeps us from walking in light. He identifies this problem as indwelling sin (1:5-10). If we are unaware of its nature or unwilling to deal with it, our fellowship with God breaks down. Second, he deals with the *provision* that allows us to walk in the light (2:1-11). Christ's sacrificial death and sinless life are God's means of grace to keep us in the light. Third, John points out an ever-present *peril* to fellowship with God (2:12-17). This is worldliness, which can be a problem for any Christian.

Living in God's Family Means Anticipating the Future (2:18—3:24)

This section offers several reminders of the imminence of Christ's return. We live in the "last hour" (2:18) and at any time the absent master may return (3:2-3). This, in itself, is an incentive to holy living.

Anticipating the future also has two additional components. First, to be ready for Christ's return, we must have *right belief* (2:18-27); in other words, we must guard against false teaching and protect the truth. At the same time, living for the future necessitates *right behavior* (2:28—3:24). Here, John identifies righteousness and love as behavior characterizing a life that is ready for the Second Coming.

Living in God's Family Means Believing in His Name (4:1—5:21)

The idea of correct belief is particularly evident in the final third of 1 John. We are told, for instance,

that we are not to believe every spirit (4:1) and that
we are to rely on (believe) the love God has for us
(4:16). Similarly, the one who believes that Jesus is
the Christ is born of God (5:1) and becomes a vic-
torious overcomer (5:5).

John links belief with two concepts that already
have surfaced in this book: *love* and *life.* He begins
by explaining that our love must be *discerning.* We
are to have compassion and reach out to others—but
that does not mean we are to be gullible and believe
every notion that comes along (4:1-6). He then
shows us that our love is to be *supernatural.* It is a
quality derived from God's character, since we read
that "God is love" (4:8). This supernatural element is
explored fully in 4:7-12. Finally, John explains that
our love is a *perfected* love. It is demonstrated in
history but comes to full fruition in us (4:13-21).

The concept of life as it pertains to correct belief is
emphasized in chapter 5. Here, we discover the
characteristics of life (5:1-5); the *certainty* of life and
how we can be sure it is ours as a present possession
(5:6-12); and some *consequences* of this assurance
(5:13-21).

Based on this extended breakdown, the outline of
John's first epistle looks like this:

Introduction 1:1-4
  I. WALKING IN THE LIGHT
     (1:5—2:17)
     A. The Problem (1:5-10)
     B. The Provision (2:1-11)
     C. The Peril (2:12-17)
 II. LIVING FOR THE FUTURE
     (2:18—3:34)
     A. We Must Believe Right
        (2:18-27)

B. We Must Behave Right
   (2:28—3:24)
   (1) Righteousness (2:28—
      3:10)
   (2) Love (3:10-24)
III. BELIEVING IN HIS NAME (4:1—5:21)
   A. Believing Is Related to Love (4:1-21)
      (1) It is a discerning love
         (4:1-6)
      (2) It is a supernatural love
         (4:7-12)
      (3) It is a perfected love
         (4:13-21)
   B. Believing Is Related to Life
      (5:1-21)
      (1) The characteristics of life
         (5:1-5)
      (2) The certainty of life
         (5:6-12)
      (3) The consequences of life
         (5:13-21)

This analysis of 1 John is like a tour through a museum. We'll first stop at areas of significance to get a good look at our subject matter. Then, after we've resumed our journey, we'll return to some original exhibits to get more information, gain additional insights, or look at the display from a different vantage point. The above outline should keep us from losing our way as we do so. And, importantly, it also should show us how knowing God more fully can help us love one another more deeply.

Meeting the Author

I was on my way to meet with some of my students when a young man in his early twenties came up and introduced himself. He explained that he once had taken a correspondence course offered by a local Bible college, and that I had written one of the course's lessons. He had some questions about the material, so we spent several minutes chatting about it. As our conversation ended he said, "You know, the material means a lot more to me now that I've met the author." What does this little anecdote have to do with a study of 1 John? Well, before we look at our material, it would be beneficial to know something about its author.

This epistle is attributed to John, the beloved disciple. John is an old man, well into his eighties, as he writes and shares the wealth of his own rich life. A survey of the Gospel record, however, reveals that John was not always a model of godly behavior.

One scene, for example, depicts him as a man with an intolerant attitude. He once resisted a disciple who was not one of the Twelve. "Teacher," said John, "we saw a man casting out demons in Your name and we told him to stop, because he was not one of us." Jesus rebuked John and explained that anyone doing good in the power of Christ should be commended rather than condemned (Mark 9:38-39).

Another incident pictures John as possessing an unloving spirit. When a local town treated the apostles in an inhospitable manner, John, along with James, responded by asking Jesus, "Lord, do You want us to call fire down from heaven and destroy them?" (Luke 9:54) It was not without reason that Jesus called John one of the "Sons of Thunder" (Mark 3:17). Yet here, Jesus rebukes the man who was to become the Apostle of Love for his *lack* of love.

A third scene depicts John as possessing unbridled ambition. In Mark's Gospel, John and James approach Christ and ask for a privileged place in the coming

kingdom, specifically, the seats to His right and left.
Jesus says this request is one that only the Father can
fulfill. He also suggests they do not know what they
are asking for. A true leader does not grasp for power,
but becomes the servant of all.

Apparently, John matured quickly, for in the Gospels he becomes one of "the inner three" who are
privy to special events in Christ's life (Mark 5:37;
9:2). In fact, Christ has enough confidence in John to
entrust His mother to him (John 19:25-27). John
later is recognized as a leader in the early church
(Acts 3:1-11; 4:1-4). When last we see the Apostle, he
is in exile on the Island of Patmos (Rev. 1:9). Tradition tells us he lived to a very old age and was buried
at Ephesus. By then, his life clearly had become a
fitting human instrument to convey the truth of this
epistle.

Having met the author, let us now explore his
work.

1 John 1:1-4

[1]That which was from the beginning, which we have heard, which we have seen with our eyes, which we have looked at and our hands have touched—this we proclaim concerning the Word of life. [2]The life appeared; we have seen it and testify to it, and we proclaim to you the eternal life, which was with the Father and has appeared to us. [3]We proclaim to you what we have seen and heard, so that you also may have fellowship with us. And our fellowship is with the Father and with His Son, Jesus Christ. [4]We write this to make our joy complete.

2 Our Message and Its Meaning

Last spring, my wife Helen spent ten days in the hospital recovering from surgery. During her confinement, well-meaning friends sent Helen cards wishing her a speedy recovery and assuring her of their love and concern. A few of the well-wishers even followed up their message in a concrete way. They put in a personal appearance at the hospital.

God also has shared a message of great encouragement with us. And, apart from simply sending us this message—important as that is—He, too, has put in a personal appearance with the visit of His Son. John describes the uniqueness of this message and the Person whom the message declares (1:1-2). He then explains our responsibility to this message and the results of our responsibility (vv. 3-4).

The Message Describes a Unique Principle (1:1-2)

Three times in the epistle's first two verses, John uses the term "life." He speaks of the "Word of life" (v. 1), notes that the "life" appeared, and states "we pro-claim to you the eternal life" (v. 2). Yet there is some confusion here. In the phrase "Word of life," does the "Word" apply to Christ, or is it a reference to the Christian message? In other words, is John speaking of the person of Christ, or a proclamation about Him?

Similar expressions throughout the New Testa-ment always refer to the message. The "word of the kingdom" (Matt. 13:19, NASB) is a message about the kingdom. When Paul mentions the "word of life" (Phil. 2:16), he is talking about the message of life. Therefore, it seems best to interpret John's expres-sion as one which refers primarily to the *message* of life. However, as we will see shortly, John *indirectly* applies this phrase to Christ in one context.

This little phrase—the "Word of life"—is worth all this discussion because it is so very important. It describes what man has consistently sought after and desperately needs: life. Most persons are ready to admit that our society is characterized by people who *exist,* but who do not really *live.* Our great fear, as John Henry Newman once said, is not that life will come to an end, but that it will never have a beginning.

Christians, however, have a message which will transform the bleakness and monotony of man's exis-tence into a thing of meaning. And that message is that through Christ, all men may fully experience a new life. We need not fear each new day; we can meet it with optimism and hope. This is our mes-sage's unique principle.

In verse 2, this message of life is expanded. "Life" is described as being eternal. To many people, this phrase suggests a distant hope that becomes ours after we die. The emphasis of this verse, though, is that eternal life is a *present* possession. When I commit *my* life to Christ, God shares *His* life with me. I begin to enjoy eternal life in the here and now—not just in the sweet bye and bye.

A number of years ago, my wife and I purchased a home. According to the terms of the contract, the house would not become ours until April 1st. Yet since the former owner already had moved out, he graciously allowed us to move some of our furniture into the house a month early—even though it had not come into our full, legal ownership. We also were able to paint several rooms and do some minor renovations before the day of the final closing. We enjoyed limited use of the house before the day of full possession.

Eternal life is a great deal like my experience with that house. Eternal life is ours because we are members of God's family. We will enter into full enjoyment of that life when we go to be with the Lord. In the meantime, we still can enjoy it now. Eternal life infuses our earthly life with a sense of quality and purpose that really makes a difference.

The Message Introduces a Unique Person (1:1-2)

This message of life is more than an abstract principle. It is embodied in a real person, Jesus of Nazareth, who is God *and* man. Both Christ's deity and humanity are described for us in verses 1 and 2.

He is Divine and Eternal. Two statements in this passage describe Christ in eternity past. The first is in the opening statement of the book: "That which was from the beginning." The second is, "The eternal life, which was with the Father" (v. 2). Both refer indirectly to Christ; they tell us, first, about His relation to time, and second, about His relation with the Father.

John often uses the expression "from the beginning" in writing about the subject of pre-temporal existence. He tells us, for example, that the devil was a murderer from the beginning (John 8:44) and that Satan has been sinning from the beginning (1 John 3:8). Because of the tense used in verse 1, this phrase is best taken as referring to Christ's pre-temporal beginning. If one could stand on the rim of time and look back into eternity, Jesus Christ always was.

The phrase in verse 2 tells us something of Christ's relationship with the Father in His pre-existent state. John indicates He was with the Father. The term "with" can have a variety of meanings in everyday conversation. It can refer to an abstract relationship, as when I say, "I took my raincoat with me" or "I do business with the First National Bank." It also can mean a mere physical proximity or spatial juxtaposition, as when I state, "I was with 300 other people on a subway car."

The "with" employed in 1 John suggests more than any of these other usages. It pictures an unbroken communion and close relationship between Father and Son. It describes a face-to-face encounter that has existed between them from all eternity.

He is Human and Historical. John wants to show us that in Jesus Christ, the eternal has entered history. The string of verbs he uses reinforce this truth:

- We have *heard*
- We have *seen*
- We have *looked at*
- Our hands have *touched* (1:1).

Taken together, all four statements stress Christ's complete identification with the human race. He is more than a divine visitor. His human body was attuned to every human sense. He took our human likeness in every way and identified with the human race—not just for a time, but for all eternity.

Christ did not live on earth in a hermetically sealed container, but faced physical exhaustion, hunger, and thirst (Luke 4:2). He suffered the same ridicule and opposition we do when we try to serve God in the world (Matt. 13:57). He was tempted in the same areas that we are (Heb. 4:15).

Christians have no difficulty accepting the humanity of Christ, but we often ignore this fact or minimize its implications. In our efforts to guard Jesus' deity, we have made His humanity irrelevant. The heavenly origin of Jesus *is* important. Yet we forget that He left real footprints on the seashore. We forget that real blood stained the ground at the foot of the cross.

The Message Has Unique Purposes (1:3-4)

Three words in verses 3 and 4 sum up the reasons why God has entrusted the message of life to us. They reveal the unique purposes of this message. The first word is "proclaim"; it describes the purpose of our message for the world. The second is "fellowship"; it suggests the purpose of our relations with others in the family of God. The third is "joy"; it describes the purpose for our life. Together, these words show us how we are to live as believers and outline our responsibilities to the message of life.

Purpose One: Proclamation. "I advise the church to declare a moratorium on preaching for the next two years." I heard these words over my car radio as I listened to a local talk show personality. He was explaining why he was disenchanted with Christianity. Basically, he felt the church was long on words and short on deeds. He suggested that Christians stop talking until they could establish better credibility in the world through their actions. Only then could the church take up the business of preaching again.

I must admit that I found a measure of truth in his caustic comments. In some places the church *has* lost its right to be heard. Our actions often have failed to conform to our words. As a result, a credibility gap has emerged between Christians and society. However, I do not believe that silence is the answer to this problem. Rather, we must continue to couple our presence in the world with a clear proclamation of truth. Proclamation and presence go hand in hand. As Christians, we have a responsibility to verbally bear witness to the message of life, and to support our words with the testimony of our lives.

The thought of being a witness, however, paralyzes some Christians. We visualize a witness as someone who has all the answers and who meets objections with appropriate quotations of Scripture. The hapless unbeliever is bludgeoned into silence by the witness' competent use of suitable verses.

It should be pointed out, though, that there's a considerable difference between being a witness and being a lawyer. A lawyer argues his case, marshals his arguments, and prepares effective rebuttals. In this way, he hopes to settle a legal argument in favor of his client.

A witness, on the other hand, is one who has information he is willing to share with others. He need not possess any outstanding qualifications apart from that. He simply needs to tell others, clearly and personally, what he's experienced. A witness who has vital information and withholds it commits a criminal act. It is a witness' responsibility to come forward and disclose what he knows. The same is true with the Christian message.

Another distorted view pictures a witness as a person who uses the "hit-and-run approach." The believer sits in his car with the motor running, waiting for the service station attendant to come back with change from a twenty-dollar bill. As he receives his change, the witness drops a tract into the unsuspecting attendant's hand. The Christian then drives hurriedly away before any conversation can take place.

At the other end of the spectrum we find the Christian who uses the overkill approach. This witness presses the potential convert to make a "decision," regardless of the individual's needs. He pushes for a sinner's prayer, a signed decision card, or a verbal assent to the claims being presented. He doesn't bother to see whether the person to whom he's talking really understands the Gospel.

Another approach to witnessing could be called the "Madison Avenue" technique. Here we mimic a set of mechanical steps outlined for us in witnessing manuals. We perfect our techniques and manipulate potential converts into making a "decision."

In studying Scripture, we see that Christ's witnessing techniques did not follow any of these patterns. He met people at their point of need; obviously, that point was different for different people. Yet He inevitably led them to a recognition of their sin and to a realization that He could deal with it. Note Jesus' lack of uniformity as He speaks to people such as Nicodemus (John 3:1-21), the woman at the well (John 4:1-26), Zaccheus (Luke 19:1-9), and the rich young ruler (Matt. 19:16-30). Jesus does not use a stereotyped approach or pat formula, yet He is an incredibly effective witness. When He speaks, people abandon the kingdom of darkness and make their way into the kingdom of light.

Witnessing should be a natural activity for us as well. When we share sufficient information to enable the Holy Spirit to convict men of their sin, changes will result.

Purpose Two: Fellowship. The term "fellowship" means to share something in common or to have a powerful common interest. Two or three fanatical football fans glued to a 26-inch color TV screen are enjoying fellowship. A group of suburban housewives who meet each Tuesday morning for a fitness class also are committed to a common cause and are experiencing a fellowship of sorts.

Christians too are bound together in a common cause. We aren't united because we happen to live together in one geographical location. We aren't united because we belong to a similar social stratum or ethnic group. Rather, it is because we possess a common life in Jesus Christ that we can share fellowship with one another.

A brief study of the word "fellowship" reveals that this term means more than coffee and doughnuts in the church basement. We can summarize the characteristics of true fellowship in four observations:

(1) Fellowship is two-dimensional. John begins by describing fellowship on the horizontal level—that is, relationships between believers. He speaks of *you* having fellowship with *us*. He then observes that our fellowship also is with the Father and His Son, Jesus Christ. This describes the vertical aspect of fellowship (v. 3).

It is important to note that our horizontal relationships in the Christian life cannot be separated from our vertical one. This theme is emphasized throughout the epistle. In fact, the test of our vertical relationship with God is seen in the tangible, horizontal relationships we maintain with other Christians. If my relationship with God is shallow and shaky, I should not be surprised if my relationships with other Christians are lacking in integrity. Deep personal relationships with God's people come from a healthy relationship with God Himself. The visible is the test of the invisible. This is a key to maintaining love in God's family.

(2) Fellowship with the Father cannot be divorced from fellowship with the Son. This is clear from the statement, "Our fellowship is with the Father and with His Son, Jesus Christ" (v. 3). Our relationship to the first Member of the Trinity cannot be separated from the second. This is a truth to which the epistle returns more than once. In approaching the Father, it is impossible to bypass the Son. Some of John's opponents, however, taught that one could have a mystical relationship with the Father directly; thus, the Son was not necessary for access to God.

A similar belief is seen in some contemporary religious circles. Varieties of eastern mysticism claim that deep, inner meditation can enable a devotee to reach God directly. Yet this verse in 1 John clearly indicates that the only way to the Father is through the Son. To relinquish one is to lose the other.

(3) Fellowship involves a close relationship with people. We sometimes hear people say it is difficult to "get close" to a certain individual, that so-and-so has an abrasive personality, that it's hard to like him or her. Yet as we saw a moment ago, a fundamental part of being a member of God's family involves our ability to get close to one another. Being a Christian means we cannot hold people at arm's length. We must be open to each other and recognize that part of our responsibility to the message of life is a willingness to share ourselves. That is a key to learning

how to love God's family.

(4) Fellowship involves a sharing of resources. The resources we share may be spiritual in nature. We read, for instance, that the early Christians continued in the Apostles' doctrine and that their fellowship included praying with one another (Acts 2:42).

In addition to these spiritual aspects, fellowship involves a sharing of material provisions. The early church shared its possessions and distributed them as each one had need (Acts 2:45). It is significant that the word "sharing" also is used to describe the distribution of financial aid mentioned in the Book of Galatians (6:6).

The notion of fellowship, then, involves sharing, whether it be of a material or spiritual nature. The fellowship John anticipates for his readers includes both factors.

Purpose Three: Joy. John covets joy for his readers as well as for himself (v. 4). In the fourth Gospel he repeatedly refers to joy as a trait all believers should possess. And what characterizes this joy?

John's first thought is that our joy is to be continuous—and remain that way. It is more than a momentary, psychological high. It is a deep and abiding experience which does not evaporate when adverse circumstances come our way. The second characteristic of joy is that it is complete. It lacks nothing. The joyous Christian is as glad as he possibly can be.

Our model for this joy is found in Christ Himself. Christ tells His disciples that He wants *His* Joy to be in them, and for it to be "complete" (John 15:11). In other words, *His* joy is identical to the joy *we* are to experience. We are to possess the joy of Christ.

Does that mean, therefore, that we're always to walk around with jolly faces? On the contrary. Christ did not walk around with a broad grin artificially pasted to His face. He experienced times of difficulty and anguish—as the scene in the Garden of Gethsemane reveals. His behavior there was far removed from the giddy smiles and superficial laughter which many Christians feel ought to be a standard part of the believer's makeup. And yet, though He faced death, Christ still could feel a deep sense of joy. Why? Because He was in God's will—despite mental turmoil and physical pain. It was due to the "joy set before Him [that He] endured the cross" (Heb. 12:2).

To possess this type of joy is a priceless commodity. And in his writings, John gives several guidelines to ensure that we experience it.

(1) Unbroken fellowship. If we lack complete and continuous joy, we need to check up on our fellowship with the Father and His Son. Only when this relationship is healthy, only when our fellowship with God is unbroken, will our joy be a reality.

(2) Unquestioned obedience. Christ also relates joy to obedience (John 15:10-11). The believer's obedience to Christ is to be patterned after Christ's obedience to the Father. Unquestioned loyalty and a devotion to the Father's will characterized the Saviour's obedience. As we already have seen, His obedience often was worked out in times of great stress and difficulty. But such obedience will create joy in us, as it did in Him.

(3) Answered prayer. In John's Gospel, Christ speaks of the disciples' present sorrow in contrast to their future joy. After the Resurrection, joy would be theirs and nothing could take it away from them; their joy would be maintained because of their access to God in prayer. "Ask and you will receive, and your joy will be complete" (John 16:24). This promise clearly applies to modern-day readers as well.

All three of the factors undergird John's words

concerning joy in verse 4 of this epistle.

John has introduced us to the three great purposes of the message of life: proclamation, fellowship, and joy. These purposes remind us that we have obligations to people both inside and outside the family of God. Parents occasionally need to remind children of their family responsibilities. John has done the same for us.

1 John 1:5-10

[5]This is the message we have heard from Him and declare to you: God is light; in Him there is no darkness at all. [6]If we claim to have fellowship with Him yet walk in the darkness, we lie and do not live by the truth. [7]But if we walk in the light, as He is in the light, we have fellowship with one another, and the blood of Jesus, His Son, purifies us from every sin. [8]If we claim to be without sin, we deceive ourselves and the truth is not in us. [9]If we confess our sins, He is faithful and just and will forgive us our sins and purify us from all unrighteousness. [10]If we claim we have not sinned, we make Him out to be a liar and His word has no place in our lives.

3 Communication Breakdowns

Most marriages today are in trouble—and we've developed a slew of theories to explain why. Psychologists have spent years cataloging the prime causes of marital breakups. They've identified such various problems as finances, infidelity, and simple boredom with one's spouse.

Yet one item, interestingly, seems to appear at the top of every marriage counselor's list: a lack of ability, or lack of desire, to communicate. These are, in fact, problems that can infect an entire family. Teenagers complain they can't have meaningful discussions with their parents. Husbands and wives live under the same roof for years and never say anything more substantive to one another than, "Please pass the butter," or "Are you finished with the business section of the paper?"

Communication breakdowns can create problems in our spiritual life, as well. In verses 3 and 4, John examined the deep fellowship and full joy that should characterize every Christian's life. Yet we must admit that our own spiritual experience usually does not measure up to those ideals. Our joy is absent, our fellowship less than real. God seems light-years away and the daily frustrations of life blunt the sharp edge of our Christianity. So we convince ourselves that our condition is a temporary mood; if we can just wait it out, the feeling will pass.

The source of our malaise, though, may be more serious. It *could* signal that a communication breakdown has developed between God and ourselves. And in this portion of his epistle, John covers the probable cause of this breakdown: sin.

Sin is deceptive. We are prone to be less than honest about it—both with God and ourselves. In these verses, John weaves his remarks about sin around three false claims people often make. These false statements are as follows:

If we claim to have fellowship with Him, yet walk in darkness...	Verse 6
If we claim to be without sin...	Verse 8
If we claim we have not sinned...	Verse 10

In a way, these statements are like the flashing red light on your car's dashboard; they're an outward signal of an inner problem—a problem that requires immediate corrective maintenance. John therefore explores the philosophy behind these statements and examines the consequences of each one.

Claim One: False Claims to Fellowship (1:5-7)

John explains that people who claim to have a close walk with God—yet who actually live in sin—have an inadequate understanding of the Christian message. This is especially true in terms of their understanding of God. Weak views of sin usually start with weak views of Him. John thus provides us with a clear message about God; he then proceeds to outline the implications of that message.

The Message Is Presented.

(1) The source is divine (v. 5). John reminds us that the source of this message comes from Christ, who, of all persons, is best qualified to tell us about God's character.

When a person receives a crucial message, he usually checks several sources to make sure the news is authentic. If a source is unreliable, the message may be treated with suspicion. But sources tested and found reliable can be counted on to provide trustworthy information.

Such is the case with information about God. People sometimes accept facts about God without checking their sources. Information about Him may be passed subtly through the media (which normally give the God of the Bible a bad press). Other images of Him come from parents or ourselves. As a result, the God we perceive may be a God of our own making. Psychologists are partially correct in stating that "God" often is nothing more than a father figure or the projection of our own desires.

A concept of God based on such perceptions *will* be erroneous. Yet Christians have an authentic and reliable knowledge of God. Why? Because our source is "God the only Son, who is at the Father's side, [who] has made Him known" (John 1:18).

(2) The subject is divine (1 John 1:5-7). One fact is emphasized here regarding God's divine nature: He is light. This truth is stated positively, "God is light"; and then negatively, "In Him there is no darkness at all."

This "light" analogy teaches two truths—that God is morally perfect, and that He is self-revealing. It therefore tells us something about who God *is* (holy and flawless) and what He *does* (reveals Himself).

The idea of God being light without one bit of darkness speaks of God's perfection and flawless nature from a moral point of view. Christians forget the significance of this fact when painful situations enter their lives. At such times, it is easy to charge God with sinister motives or to feel that He has been devious and unfair with us. Yet if God is light and perfectly flawless, such charges are not only inaccurate, but absurd.

The other truth described here is that God is self-revealing. God, unlike man, is completely open and transparent to us. We tend to hide our true selves, fearing that people will gain a distorted picture of us or not like what they see. This is not the case with God. The marvels of nature, His mighty acts in history, and the inspired Scriptures show us God as He really is.

The Moral Implications Are Presented. The message of God's character revealed in verse 5 leads naturally into a discussion of how His character relates to our sin. Simply stated, people who perceive God properly will understand sin better.

Years ago, I worked as a waiter in a summer resort. Each waiter was responsible for polishing a set of drinking glasses and placing them face down at a table setting. An overly conscientious dining room hostess monitored our work and reprimanded us if the glasses were not sparkling clean. To inspect the glass, she held it up to the brilliant light of a crystal chandelier hanging in the center of the dining hall. Exposed to the brilliance of the light, smudged fingerprints and water stains became painfully obvious.

God is the self-revealing light who performs the same function in our lives. If I dared to hold my life up to His perfect holiness and flawless character, my own imperfection and sin would be exposed. This truth about God's character introduces John's discussion of sin in verses 6 and 7. John treats the moral implications of this message about God in both a negative and positive fashion.

(1) The negative description (v. 6). This verse examines the statement, "If we claim to have fellowship with Him, yet walk in darkness. . . . "

As we've already seen, the person who makes this claim has a faulty understanding of both God and sin. The real test of our relationship with God is not what we *say,* but where we *live.* If I claim my best friend and I both live in Toronto, yet everyone knows he really lives in Miami, my claim does not fit the facts. If a person claims he lives with God in the light, yet his address is in the darkness, he obviously does not have a close relationship with God.

Many Christians make such false claims without even realizing it. We have a desire to impress others with our spirituality. We want people to feel that our relationship with God is closer than it really is. So we drop hints about the length of time we spend in prayer, or the number of people to whom we've witnessed. Our peers may be impressed, but if we are speaking empty words, God will see through us. Consequently, John warns us to weigh our words and to guard against irresponsible statements concerning our Christian life.

(2) The positive description (v. 7). There is an alternative to living in darkness. It is living in the light as God is in the light. Since God lives in the light, we may have fellowship with Him—if we make a conscious and sustained effort to live a life in conformity to His character. The results of such efforts are twofold.

First, we will have fellowship with one another. The expression "one another" refers not to God and ourselves, but to ourselves and other Christians. The use of this term in John's epistles always refers to fellow believers (3:11, 23; 4:7, 11-12; 2 John 5). Here again, John is stressing the need for good relations among members of God's family. Without such relationships, our witness to the world will be ineffectual.

The second result is that Christ's blood will cleanse us from all sin. What could be a more positive description of the results of walking in the light?

Claim Two: Denial of the Sin Principle (1:8-9)

The false claims of verses 8 ("If we claim to be without sin") and 10 ("If we claim we have not sinned") appear to be quite similar. Yet there *is* a difference between them. Verse 8 recognizes sin as a *principle;* verse 10 treats sin as an *act.* For the sake of clarity, we'll discuss John's analysis of sin in verse 8, examine the remedy to sin identified in verse 9, and then look at John's treatment of sinful acts in verse 10.

The Problems of Eradication and Sophistication. The false claim of verse 8—which, in effect, denies man's sinful nature—can be made in more than one way. One approach is to claim man *had* a sinful nature, but lost it. Some theologians contend that after conversion, man's sinful nature is eradicated through an act of total sanctification. God extracts the sin nature like a diseased tooth; this troublesome part of our nature is gone and will bother us no more. This claim to sinlessness, however, contradicts John's statement here. If we claim to be without sin, we deceive ourselves.

Most Christians, fortunately, do not accept the theology of eradication. They willingly concede that sin is a permanent part of our nature. Yet many believers *do* fall into the trap of verse 8 in another way.

Regrettably, we are surrounded by a society that denies sin as a *concept.* We have become too "sophisticated" or "enlightened" to believe in so archaic a notion as sin. Intelligent people abandoned this concept about the time they discovered the earth was not flat.

This type of thinking has infected modern educational models, psychological principles, and political theories. Christians are confronted daily by a society which touts the essential goodness of man and his ability to invariably make correct ethical choices. Christians, therefore, must be discriminating in what they read and accept. It is important that we do not embrace a model of man and sin which differs from the biblical one.

Confession as a Remedy (v. 9). The proper response to verse 8 is to acknowledge that such false claims are sinful in and of themselves and thus, need to be confessed. The cure for the claims of verses 8 and 10 is the same: confession of sin.

The word "confession" means literally, "to say the same thing." Confession can be defined, then, as accepting God's spiritual diagnosis of our sinful condition.

A person goes to the doctor and takes a series of tests. The physician asks a barrage of questions, both about the patient's present health and his past history. Then the moment comes. The doctor shares his medical diagnosis with the patient. If the diagnosis is disturbing and major surgery is called for, the patient may be tempted to doubt the doctor's word. Perhaps a mistake has been made with his tests. The doctor may be mistaken in his prognosis. At this point, the patient essentially is denying the physician's evaluation. The doctor's conclusions are too unsettling and painful.

God also probes the spiritual life of His children and shares His diagnosis with them. If I don't like what I hear, I'll seek to minimize the seriousness of His report. Such a response, however, constitutes a refusal to confess my sin. I am refusing to accept God's diagnosis of my condition. But when I *do* evaluate my behavior as God does, I immediately know what my response must be: confession. Then God can reach out to me in cleansing and forgiveness.

Having stated this, two further observations need to be made about confession, and two more about forgiveness.

(1) Confession must be concrete. To confess my sin, I must do more than ask forgiveness in a general way at the end of each day. I must do more than hope that a glib statement will cover all my negative behavior. Confession involves being specific about individual acts or attitudes of disobedience.

Picture an individual presenting himself at police headquarters. He confesses that he has broken the law. Since he is a criminal, he tells the officer behind the desk that he ought to be locked up. The police sergeant asks the lawbreaker to be more specific about his crime. Has he robbed a bank, stolen a car, committed a murder? The crime cannot be dealt with unless the individual is specific in his confession.

Spiritual confession also involves a willingness to talk about specific sinful behavior, attitudes, and situations. Only as I am specific about such matters can God help me and offer His pardoning grace.

(2) Confession is continual. Confession must be habitual if fellowship is to have any significance. It must take place daily as the voice of the Spirit points out areas of disobedience and weakness. To let sinful matters slide is to compound the problem.

A consumer may use his credit card indiscriminately and not take care of the debts he is assuming. Over a period of time, though, these debts will accumulate and create serious financial crises. His account may even be turned over to a collection agency. But if his debts are dealt with systematically, he can avoid such problems.

In dealing with sin, we must avoid an "expense account" approach. An old slogan asserts, "Keep short accounts with God." That truth certainly is applicable here. If we deal with our spiritual debts on a consistent basis, God will not have to take radical steps to bring us to Himself.

(3) Forgiveness is complete. John claims two things happen when we confess our sin. First, God forgives—or puts away—our sins. Second, He cleanses us from them (v. 9).

My youngest son occasionally used to spill his milk at the supper table. A flood of tears and deep remorse normally followed. I'd comfort him and tell him he needn't be disturbed. All was forgiven. While this helped cheer him up a little, something else needed to be done as well. Someone had to clean up the spilt milk. Both forgiveness *and* cleansing were required. As our Heavenly Father, God graciously does both of these things as soon as we confess our sin.

In verse 9, the little word "all" should not be overlooked. We are forgiven and cleansed from *all* unrighteousness. No sin is so trivial that God overlooks it. No trespass is so serious that God will not forgive it. He treats every sin in the same fashion and is willing to completely forgive all.

(4) Forgiveness is certain. What if I confess my sin and God refuses to forgive me? This fear usually can be traced to our experiences with forgiveness on the human plane. One Christian confesses to another, but forgiveness is not forthcoming. The wronged party has been hurt so deeply that bitterness has marred the relationship. He cannot bring himself to forgive his brother.

John affirms that such a situation will never occur in God's dealings with His family. The Apostle uses two words to emphasize that His forgiveness is certain: "faithful" and "just" (v. 9). The term "faithful" means God is dependable. His veracity is at stake and thus He can be counted on to do what He says He will. He will never go back on His word.

"Just" means that God deals with the debt of our sin honestly and fairly. A man promises his wife that he'll take her on a winter vacation to Hawaii. He feels bound to honor his promise. Unfortunately, he is short of cash. So he resorts to unscrupulous business practices and cheats others out of their money. He has been faithful to the promise made to his wife; yet he was not just or fair in the way he kept it. God deals with our sin in a way that is faithful to His promise, but which also is fair and righteous. This is assured, as we'll see in chapter 2, by the death of His Son.

I talked with a twenty-year-old housewife after a

Sunday morning service. "I have committed a sin that God will not forgive," she said.

"Have you confessed that sin?" I asked, explaining to her what confession really meant. She indicated that she had indeed confessed it many times, but was certain God had not forgiven her. I opened the New Testament and read 1 John 1:9.

She looked at the verse without comment and sat silently for several moments. Then she responded, "I was wrong. My problem is not that *God* refuses to forgive me. My problem is I cannot forgive *myself.*"

This woman's feelings are not unique. Many of us have difficulty forgiving ourselves, especially if the sin is habitual. God truly has forgiven us, but we do not *feel* forgiven. This situation is somewhat like the salvation experience. Our salvation is not primarily a case of feeling, but of fact. I am or am not a Christian depending on whether I have accepted God's grace. The same is true with forgiveness. I may not feel forgiven, but that does not alter the objective fact of God's forgiveness—providing I have met His condition of confession. If God truly has forgiven me, I need to ask Him to help me forgive myself. In this way, my feelings can catch up with what is objectively true.

Claim Three: Denial of Sinful Acts (1:10)

Nature of the Claim. John now comes to the final claim of this chapter: If we say we have not sinned, we make God a liar. The issue here is not sin as a general principle, but sin as a specific act.

This claim grows out of the teaching of the previous verse. John has spoken of the need for confession and the certainty of cleansing. We might respond by stating that we do not need this provision. *Others* may need it, be *we* certainly don't. At this point, we not only are fooling ourselves, but are casting doubt on God's Word as well.

It is easier to ignore sin than it is to confess it. David lived with his sin for many months before confessing it in Nathan's presence (2 Samuel 11— 12). Did he think that if he evaded the sin, it would go away? Or did he feel that as King, he was entitled to special privileges and was beyond the law? On both counts, he would have been wrong.

Rationalization is another approach. We begin to formulate excuses: "I really had no choice. I *had* to sin."

"There were extenuating circumstances. I couldn't have done anything else."

"Everybody is doing it. Don't blame me."

"It wasn't my fault. God never should have let me get into this mess."

Or, I may choose to minimize my sin. God speaks to me about my short temper. He convicts me regarding my lack of truthfulness. I may admit that I am not perfect in these areas; but at the same time, I don't want to agree completely with God and see the sin as He does. So I admit that I *sometimes* lose my temper. Once in a while, I lie a *little*.

Results of the Claim. In verse 8, we noted the effect of these false claims as they relate to *us;* we deceive ourselves and are devoid of the truth. Here, in verse 10, we see the results of these claims in relation to *God;* He is made a liar because I repudiate what He says. God calls me a sinner and I choose to disagree with Him. If God's Word were in me, I would not play such games. I would accept His evaluation of my moral condition without question.

If I find myself caught in this trap, I should check up on my understanding of the Word. If I take it seriously, I will not argue with God. I will confess my sin openly as He reveals it to me. I will accept His evaluation as legitimate. If I affirm what God says about my behavior, I then can experience the joy of forgiveness. A life of fellowship with Him will become a reality.

How does all this relate to loving God's family? Simply stated, the inner tensions currently plaguing the body of Christ are undeniably related to sin. Our false claims and lack of confession keep us separated from God and fellow believers. By insisting on our own spirituality, we are prevented from having genuine fellowship.

Only when we acknowledge the true dimensions of sin and appropriate its remedy can we become free to love. Then the barriers will fall. Then we can love one another as members of God's family.

1 John 2:1-11

¹My dear children, I write this to you so that you will not sin. But if anybody does sin, we have one who speaks to the Father in our defense—Jesus Christ, the Righteous One. ²He is the atoning sacrifice for our sins, and not only for ours but also for the sins of the whole world. ³We know that we have come to know Him if we obey His commands. ⁴The man who says, "I know Him," but does not do what He commands is a liar, and the truth is not in him. ⁵But if anyone obeys His word, God's love is truly made complete in him. This is how we know we are in Him: ⁶Whoever claims to live in Him must walk as Jesus did. ⁷Dear friends, I am not writing you a new command but an old one, which you have had since the beginning. This old command is the message you have heard. ⁸Yet I am writing you a new command; its truth is seen in Him and you, because the darkness is passing and the true light is already shining. ⁹Anyone who claims to be in the light but hates his brother is still in the darkness. ¹⁰Whoever loves his brother lives in the light, and there is nothing in him to make him stumble. ¹¹But whoever hates his brother is in the darkness and walks around in the darkness; he does not know where he is going, because the darkness has blinded him.

4 It's the
Real Thing

The words of the familiar commercial drummed their way into my subconscious. As I sat listening to my car radio, a chorus of youthful singers extolled the virtues of a soft drink which was, they promised, "the real thing." The ad's message seemed simple: Finally, here's something real, something you really can be sure of. On a hot summer day, a frosty bottle of Coke will quench your thirst. Your dreams of finding refreshment can become a reality.

Reality. Isn't that a commodity we all desire? We know only too well that our world is full of phoniness. We see hypocrisy in interpersonal relationships and dishonesty in the marketplace. We expect more of the church, but even there, we sometimes feel shortchanged.

How, then, can we encourage reality in the church? How can we learn to minister to each other in genuine ways? These are the questions we must ask of God's family. Are we merely going through the motions, or is our faith "the real thing"? This is John's concern in 2:1-11.

His line of thought here is fairly clear. The Apostle explains that God has made a provision which will enable us to live lives of integrity; this provision for real living is based on the sacrificial death of Christ (vv. 1-2). He then points out that God has given us a pattern for a genuine kind of living; this pattern is based on the sinless life of Christ (vv. 3-11).

The Sacrificial Death of Christ (2:1-2)

It is important to note that John discusses the significance of Christ's death *before* he proceeds to examine Christ's life. We never can follow the pattern of His sinless life until we appropriate the merits of His sin-cleansing death.

An indignant parishioner marched up to Miner Stearns, a great Bible teacher of a past generation. "I take exception to what you said today in Bible class," the parishioner exclaimed.

"What did you disagree with?" Stearns asked.

"You said I cannot get to heaven by following Christ's example. But I know there is a verse in the Bible that says Christ left an example and we are to follow it."

"There is indeed such a verse," replied Stearns, as he flipped through his Bible. "It is found in 1 Peter 2:21. It says Christ left an example, that we should follow His steps."

"That is exactly the verse I meant," said the parishioner. "Doesn't that contradict what you said?"

"Look at the beginning of the next verse, verse 22," Stearns replied patiently. "What does it say?"

The man read, "He committed no sin," and stopped.

"Can you follow Christ as your example there?" asked Stearns.

"Why no. I admit I have committed sin, just as everyone else."

"Then you need to appropriate the merits of His death for your sin before you follow His life as a pattern."

Like this parishioner, we also must accept Christ's death as the provision for our sin. It is a prerequisite to our taking any further steps in our walk with God. Before turning to John's study of Christ's death in verses 1b and 2, however, it would be advisable to briefly outline his concern over a correct understanding of sin.

John's Concern Over Sin

As John explains his purpose for writing, it is clear he does not want us to be either too lenient—or too severe—in our attitudes toward sin. Unfortunately, most of us react to sin in one of these two ways.

Some of us are devastated by our sin. We take a false step, fail God, and the bottom drops out of our Christian life. We brood for weeks because we have let God down. Our guilt crushes us and we cannot go on. For such people, John emphasizes the greatness of Christ's provision.

Others, by contrast, may be nonchalant in their attitudes toward sin. John already has told us that if we claim to be without sin we are deceiving ourselves (1:8). "If this is true," we reason, "what's the use? We may as well go ahead and sin." Likewise, we may feel that the greatness of God's provision means we don't need to be overly meticulous in dealing with sin. If we sin, we easily can make use of Christ's provision. John is careful, therefore, to point out, "I write this to you so that you will not sin" (2:1).

Anyone who's ever been in a plane poised for takeoff has heard a short speech about the aircraft's safety features. A stewardess explains that the passengers are safe, but in the event of an emergency, oxygen masks are available in a ceiling compartment.

Obviously, by announcing that the passengers have oxygen masks, the stewardess isn't trying to encourage the pilot to take unnecessary risks. Rather, her speech is designed to reassure the passengers that a provision has been made should an accident take place. This is John's point. He hopes we will not need God's provision for sin. But if a spiritual accident *does* take place, a provision already has been made.

The Divine Provision

A discussion of Christ's provision for sin—His death—is introduced in two phrases found in the opening verses of chapter 2. The first statement is, "We have one who speaks to the Father in our defense." The second is, "He is the atoning sacrifice for our sins."

This first phrase indicates that we have an advocate with the Father who will represent us in His presence. The Greek word John uses here is *parakletos,* which he also uses in his Gospel to describe the work of the Holy Spirit (John 14:16, 26; 16:7). In those verses, *parakletos* is translated as "counselor," and describes the work of the Holy Spirit. Like a prosecuting attorney, the Spirit shows us we are condemned in the areas of sin, righteousness, and judgment.

In 1 John 2:1, however, the Paraclete is Christ. His ministry relates to believers rather than unbelievers—as the use of the term "children" indicates. And here, Christ acts as a defense attorney vindicating us against attack, rather than as a prosecutor condemning us before the Father.

While it is true that Christ pleads our case before God, this does not mean He is trying to win over a cold-hearted judge. It is a loving Father to whom the Son speaks. The Father also has a special interest in us because we are His children. He is not merely a feelingless autocrat who insists that the demands of the law be met.

Similarly, the advocate who acts on our behalf is not a slick lawyer who uses debating skills or dubious legal loopholes to get us cleared. He is "Jesus Christ, the Righteous One" (v. 1) and so will always act in fairness. He does not plead our moral worth. He does not parade our good deeds or offer character references so the judge will release us. He does not grant assurances that our sin will never happen again. He pleads on the basis that His death atones for my sin. That fact is enough.

This brings us to the second phrase describing the divine provision: "He is the atoning sacrifice for our sins" (v. 2). The word John uses here often is translated, "propitiation"—which means Christ has reached a satisfactory settlement with the Father concerning my sin. If a drunken driver with no insurance crashes into your new car, a settlement must be reached that is proportionate to the damages incurred. In the same way, our sin has dishonored God and impugned His holy character. Yet satisfaction is rendered through Christ's atoning sacrifice.

This fact has a number of implications for Christians. For one, we will never have to pay for our own sins. Christ already has done so. A useful analogy should help to illustrate this point.

In pioneer days, when settlers roamed the prairies, grass fires often swept the plains. These enormous fires threatened the destruction of everything that crossed their path. To protect lives and possessions, the pioneers developed an ingenious plan. When smoke in the distance signaled an approaching fire, they deliberately burned a huge circle in the grass and moved themselves and their wagons to its center. Flames would approach and lick the rim of the circle, but since a fire already had burned there, the flames could not go across that ground again.

The ground at the foot of the cross is a great deal like that circle. The fire of God's wrath already has fallen there. Anyone who stands in that circle is safe from the judgment of God.

It's possible to examine at least one other implication of God's forgiveness presented here in verse 2. Picture yourself mailing a check for what you believe will satisfy an outstanding debt. A few days later, your creditor returns your check, uncashed. He informs you that your debt already is covered in full. You do not owe a penny. If your creditor is happy with this settlement, you should be also.

God sees the sacrifice of Christ as totally adequate for the sins of the world. Therefore, if God is happy with the settlement He has made concerning my sin, I should be satisfied as well. I need to rest assured in that truth. The words of a familiar hymn sum up this fact:

> Lord I believe were sinners more
> Than sands upon the ocean shore
> Thou hast for all a ransom paid
> For all a full atonement made.

The Sinless Life of Christ (2:3-11)

Almost thirty years ago, an elderly man placed a novel in my hands. It was entitled *In His Steps,* and told the story of a group of people who decided to embrace Christ's commands in a serious way. Before these believers made any decisions pertaining to business or family matters, they'd asked the penetrating question, "What would Jesus do if He were in my situation?" That question transformed their lives and brought revival to their town. The author of the novel, Charles Sheldon, presented a vital biblical truth: We must follow Christ's example and seek to imitate His ways if we are to have true life.

This truth is explored in 1 John 2:3-11. Here, John hits the nail on the head: "Whoever claims to live in Him must walk as Jesus did" (v. 6). We need to know, then, *how* Jesus lived and *what* aspects of His character we should reproduce. The answer to these questions, John explains, is twofold: we must practice obedience and we must exercise love.

The Need for Obedience (vv. 3-6). We need to be on guard against easy substitutes for obedience. At certain points in our spiritual life, we can experience great waves of emotion; our spirits soar and our feelings are touched. We shed tears or realize moments of ecstacy. Such emotional highs may be significant landmarks in our Christian experience, but they are never an alternative to obedience.

Activity also can be a cheap substitute for obeying God. We become Christian workaholics, jetting from one committee meeting to another, investing our energy in a variety of worthy projects. But all this activity could be a cover-up for a shallow commitment to Christ's commands.

Discussion also may lead us astray. We organize Bible studies and reveal our findings. We share what the statements of Scripture mean in our personal situations. Yet could our words just be a smoke screen to avoid a costly commitment to what the Scripture demands?

So what does true obedience entail? The first truth

we find is that obedience is related to assurance (v. 3). John's epistle lists a number of ways to test the reality of our faith. Obedience is one of them. By being obedient, we know that we know Christ. And when this passage speaks of knowing Christ, it is not talking about an accumulation of facts concerning a historical figure. It is describing a personal relationship between two individuals—Christ and ourselves.

The second truth is that obedience is a response to the commands of Christ (v. 4). It is tempting to discuss obedience in general terms without ever getting down to specifics. We speak of our allegiance to the commands of Christ, but become uneasy if someone asks us exactly what commands we're obeying.

We all should have definite commands we're struggling with—commands we're asking God for help in obeying.

Some Christians, though, visualize the Bible as a giant smorgasbord; we can pick commands that suit our tastes and leave ones that do not. This passage in 1 John will not allow such a luxury. The real test of obedience comes when we comply with a command we find difficult.

In April 1951, the Korean War was in full swing. As a matter of policy and strategy, President Truman had decided that United Nations troops would conduct a limited war; their goal was simply to contain communist aggression in the region. But Douglas MacArthur, who commanded the UN forces, believed the war should be pursued more vigorously. After a number of public disagreements over this issue, Truman relieved the general of his command.

Back in the United States, MacArthur was considered a hero. He explained that he only was doing his duty. He insisted on winning the war rather than achieving a truce. There was, he said, no substitute for victory. The President responded by stating that he had not fired MacArthur over a policy dispute. As commander-in-chief, Truman had given MacArthur an order; when the general refused to obey it, he was dismissed. In other words, the President implied, there was no substitute for *obedience.*

The third truth we find in these verses is that obedience cannot be divorced from love. God's love comes to maturity, or is "made complete," in the believer who is disposed to obedience (v. 5).

Every spring, my wife prepares the soil for a flower garden behind our house. Before she plants the marigolds and petunias, she adds peat moss, fertilizer, and black loam to the soil. This enriches the flower beds. When the warm weather comes, the flowers can burst out in full bloom because they are drawing these nutrients from the soil. In the same way, an obedient life is the soil that allows God's love to come to full bloom.

The final truth in these verses is that obedience to Christ's commands involves following His total lifestyle. We are to do what He says and live as He lived (v. 6).

In college, I worked part time stocking shelves at a local supermarket. The store manager was a brusque and surly individual who stood in his office surveying operations in the aisles below. He would bark out four-letter-word commands as he chomped on an unlit cigar. His presence terrorized store employees and we obeyed his commands instantly. None of us had any desire, however, to pattern our lives after him or to imitate his behavior.

Christ's example is radically different. We obey His commands *and* find in His life a model we all can strive to reproduce.

The Need for Love (vv. 7-11). Earlier, we noted that to be like Christ, we must exercise love. This command is both old and new. It is an old command because it had been with John's readers "from the beginning" (v. 7). Christ had gathered the disciples together just prior to His death and said, "A new commandment I give you: Love one another. As I have loved you, so you must love one another" (John 13:34). Six decades had passed since that time and the command that once was new now was relatively old. Christians had had it since the church began.

How, then, can this command also be new? Basically, Christians are living in a new situation. "The darkness is passing and the true light is already shining" (1 John 2:8). The death and resurrection of Christ have ushered in a new age. With it, new opportunities are presented to live out old truths.

I often hear people say that biblical truth is ancient, outdated, obsolete. Yet I believe the most contemporary truths are old commands which are lived out in new situations. This should be our constant prayer: "Lord, make the old truth new. Help me to take ancient commands, given by Christ many centuries ago, and update them. Let my friends see an old command to love become new in my life."

These verses also teach that a lack of love destroys our testimony. If we love our brother, nothing about us will make him stumble. But a lack of love can harm him (vv. 9-10). Consider the new Christian whose spiritual life already is shaky. What will he think when he sees a lack of love in older Christians? How will he react when he hears destructive gossip circulated about other members of God's family? Obviously, he will call the genuineness of our faith into question. And we should not be surprised if he is unimpressed when he sees these inconsistencies.

John's final point about love is this: a lack of love distorts our *own* vision (v. 11). Verse 10 describes the effect of this problem on others; verse 11 describes its results for ourselves. Imagine a sound sleeper who is aroused by a telephone call at 3 A.M. He gets up in the darkness and stumbles about, bumping into furniture as he tries to reach the phone.

A person devoid of love also stumbles around in darkness. He too has no clear sense of direction. Why? Because darkness blinds him to things as they really are. The believer who has hatred and harbors resentment toward another child of God has difficulty evaluating things clearly. He fails to see any positive traits in his brothers and sisters; he becomes overly critical about all phases of their life and ministry.

Ask yourself a candid question. Are you nursing bitterness against another Christian or a group of believers? Are you holding a grudge because of comments they've made or actions they have taken against you? You should think twice. This hatred will erode your spiritual life and damage you far more than it will harm others.

What can you do? Claim the truth of this passage and experience the reality of forgiveness! Resolve to be obedient to this old, yet ever-new command. It will show you how to love God's family in a much more effective manner. That's what this section of 1 John is all about.

1 John 2:12-17

[12]I write to you, dear children, because your sins have been forgiven on account of His name.

[13]I write to you, fathers, because you have known Him who is from the beginning.

I write to you, young men, because you have overcome the evil one.

I write to you, dear children, because you have known the Father.

[14]I write to you, fathers, because you have known Him who is from the beginning.

I write to you, young men, because you are strong, and the Word of God lives in you, and you have overcome the evil one.

[15]Do not love the world or anything in the world. If anyone loves the world, the love of the Father is not in him. [16]For everything in the world—the cravings of sinful man, the lust of his eyes and the boasting of what he has and does—comes not from the Father but from the world. [17]The world and its desires pass away, but the man who does the will of God lives forever.

5 Guarding against Infection

I was about to enter my friend's hospital room when a nurse stepped in front of me and barred the door. "You can't go in there," she declared. She pointed to a sign which explained that the person in this room had a contagious disease. Handing me a hospital gown and mask, she instructed me to slip them over my street clothes. Only then, looking like Marcus Welby in the operating room, was I allowed to visit my friend.

Her concern was well-founded. Every day, people become ill from minute organisms which pass unseen from one infected person to another. Often, it's possible to be in a contagious environment and not even know it.

In this epistle, John states that Christians also are exposed to a particularly contagious environment. In fact, we're exposed to a spiritual infection every time we venture into society. This infection is commonly labeled, "worldliness."

In these verses (2:12-17), John tells us who this

disease strikes, how its symptoms appear, and what steps we can take to prevent it.

The Group He Addresses (2:12-14)

The People Described. Verses 12-14 form a bridge between what John has described in verse 11 and the warning he gives concerning worldliness in verse 15. In 2:11, John referred to the problems that befall those who do not exercise love. But in doing so, he wasn't trying to upset his readers. Actually, John was describing the behavior of the *false teachers.* Now the Apostle is trying to give true Christians an assurance of what is rightfully theirs: Their sins *have* been forgiven! They have come out of the darkness into God's light (vv. 12-14).

Looking ahead to verse 15, John warns his readers not to love the world. Some commentators have concluded on the basis of that verse that the Apostle is sending this warning only to *new* Christians, since John addresses his remarks to his "dear children." The implication of such an interpretation, of course, is that spiritual veterans don't need to worry about worldliness; they've already learned how to stay clear of such temptations. But this view is not correct. John directs his remarks in verses 12-14 to *every* member of God's family. The term "children" is used elsewhere in the epistle to encompass *all* believers (2:1, 28; 3:2). The terms "fathers" and "young men" are used to differentiate levels of spiritual maturity. Thus, it is clear that John's warning about worldliness applies to all Christians.

This passage is an effective reminder that worldliness is not just a childhood disease, such as measles or mumps. Satan simply restructures temptations to keep them in line with our present desires. The things that attracted you as a young Christian may be different from the temptations that plague you today. Paul's words apply here. "If you think you are standing firm, be careful that you don't fall!" (1 Cor. 10:12)

These verses also introduce another truth: the ministry of every congregation should encompass a variety of age groups. John does not omit anyone from his pastoral concern. Neither should we. Yet some churches see themselves as ministering primarily to persons under twenty-five. Anyone over thirty should look for fellowship elsewhere. Other churches focus on reaching the "Geritol generation." They minister well to senior citizens and those approaching the golden years, but the opinions of the young are not heard and their needs are ignored.

These verses teach that no congregation can afford the luxury of ministering only to one segment of God's family. All age-groups and people in various stages of spiritual growth deserve our attention.

Finally, it is important to note that we too are the "dear children" to whom John addresses this passage. Some believers, especially those with a poor self-image, may question the reality of their faith. Apparently, many of John's readers were doing exactly that. But if a fellow believer is troubled, we need to assure him or her of God's forgiveness, as John does here.

The Benefits Conferred. Verses 12-14 describe certain privileges that members of God's family enjoy. These truths are repeated several times for emphasis. But for clarity's sake, let's look at these privileges in a threefold way.

(1) Forgiveness. Our sins have been forgiven on account of Christ's name (v. 12). We do not deserve forgiveness, nor have we earned it. It is a free gift of God.

(2) Knowledge. Three times in these verses we are reminded we have come to know Him. This is a truth we've already seen: "We know that we have come to know Him" (2:3). In that verse, as here, John is stressing the knowledge of our personal acquaintance with Christ, not theoretical information about Him. If we are members of God's family, we have been introduced to Christ in an intimate way. That relationship simply gets better with each passing day.

(3) Victory. John twice refers to the young men who have overcome the evil one (vv. 13-14). It is easy to see the defeats in our spiritual battles. We often emerge from these conflicts wounded and bleeding. It need not be that way. Christians are winners or "overcomers." We can persevere and become victors in our spiritual battles because we possess the ultimate weapon: "The Word of God lives in you" (v. 14). It is the indwelling Word that makes the difference between our being winners and losers. Just as Christ used Scripture in His battle against the evil one (Matt. 4:4), we also can rely on the Word of God. It will enable us to resist Satan and conquer the world.

The Command He Gives (2:15)

Identifying the Enemy. The aged Apostle fears that the world and its charms might victimize us. The term "world" has a vast range of meaning and a question arises here as to its exact usage. It is clear that John is not referring to the world of nature. Creation is a gift of God; though we certainly aren't to worship the physical world, we can revel in its sunsets, appreciate its scenery, and enjoy its infinite diversity (Ps. 19:1).

John also is not referring to the world of mankind. He tells us in his Gospel of God's love for all men:

"God so loved the world that He gave His one and only Son" (John 3:16). The use of the term in 1 John 2:15 must, therefore, refer to something else.

Perhaps by looking at the use of the term "world" as it used negatively throughout the epistle, we can gain an accurate understanding of its meaning here.

"The world does not know us," John claims (3:1). "Do not be surprised, my brothers, if the world hates you," he warns (3:13). "The whole world is under the control of the evil one," he concludes (5:19). What can we learn from these passages? Simply, that this "world" about which we are warned is the world controlled by Satan and organized in its rebellion against God. It represents a value system totally opposed to that of the Bible.

Worldliness is the advice of a chief accountant who encourages you to manipulate business figures to make a bigger profit. It is the suave voice of the TV announcer who says you *must* have a second car and a third television set because you deserve it. It is the pressure of our peers who say it's acceptable to sleep with someone before marriage because everyone else is doing it.

These opinions bombard us from a variety of sources. They shriek at us from the media and they whisper to us through a valued friend or close family member. We finally may decide that these pressures are too great, and so we are swept along like everyone else. But we cannot say we have not been warned. Scripture notifies us ahead of time, "Do not conform any longer to the pattern of this world, but be transformed by the renewing of your mind" (Rom. 12:2).

The second half of verse 15 highlights the importance of this command. If we love the world, we cannot love the Father. Yet how often have we seen the world's temptations lure someone away from his allegiance to God? A forty-two-year-old husband with a wife and three children recently left home to live with a younger woman. His friends couldn't understand how he found it so easy to break up his marriage. More astute observers had no trouble with this question. They realized he had been seduced. The charms of a younger woman proved irresistible. He had succumbed before he ever realized what hit him.

The same thing can happen to our spiritual commitment. The enticement of the world is so strong that we forsake our love of God for the love of things around us. Yet we fail to realize that God will not accept half of our allegiance. Some commitments must be total. Some allegiances must be unconditional. Loving God is in that category.

It was a lovely stretch of beach. The sun had just risen and the embers of the fire used to cook breakfast were growing cold. Jesus and Peter walked down the beach a few yards from the others. Three times Jesus asked, "Simon son of John, do you truly love Me more than these?" (John 21:15-17) This question must have puzzled Peter. "Love Me more than these?" To what does the "these" refer? Was Jesus referring to the disciples? To the fishing boat and its nets, still dripping from recent use?

Perhaps the question was deliberately open-ended. Perhaps it applies to us, as well. Is anything or anyone in our life receiving the love intended for God alone? *That* is the essence of worldliness. That is John's concern in 1 John 2:15.

The World and Its Components (2:16)

A more careful analysis of the world is offered to us in these verses. Here, the world is broken down into components so we can understand it more clearly and know what we are facing. These elements are cataloged for us in a threefold way: the cravings of sinful man, the lust of his eyes, and the boastings of what he has. Other translations describe these items as the lust of the flesh, the lust of the eyes, and the pride of life. Perhaps they can be understood best as the desire to have things, the desire to see things, and the desire to be somebody.

(1) The Cravings of Sinful Man. The term "craving" or "lust" refers to any desire that becomes so all-consuming that it hinders our relationship with God. Steve and Kathy have been talking about putting their house on the market and moving up to a newer, more spacious model. They have convinced themselves they must have three full baths instead of two. It's not that they really *need* the extra room, but they've compared their present home to other families' and concluded their house has fewer square feet.

Unfortunately, Steve and Kathy have begun to see their identity in terms of their possessions. Their self-worth is wrapped up in the clutter of the things they have accumulated. They no longer define their identity in terms of their relationship to Christ. They have succumbed to the cravings of sinful man. In short, they are worldly Christians.

George and Shirley have worked for a Christian organization for ten years on a meager salary. Though they regularly denounce other Christians for lusting after material possessions, this couple actually covets the same possessions for themselves. They simply cannot afford them on their limited budget.

You see, a person does not have to possess things to be worldly. Worldliness is not primarily a matter of amount, but of attitude. We can be worldly with a little or a lot. It is how we *relate* to our possessions that determines whether we've been infected.

(2) The Lust of the Eyes. This phrase suggests unlawful sexual desire. We picture someone studying a *Playboy* centerfold and allowing the activity to pollute his thought life. Such activities would fall within this area. Jesus warned, "Anyone who looks at a woman lustfully has already committed adultery with her in his heart" (Matt. 5:27). We need to take radical steps to avoid this type of sin.

Worshiping physical beauty can be a similar trap. Our society gives high marks for physical attractiveness and a handsome appearance. As a result, these attributes can become more highly regarded than inner spiritual beauty. Peter addresses this topic in his first epistle: "Your beauty . . . should be that of your inner self, the unfading beauty of a gentle and quiet spirit, which is of great worth in God's sight" (3:3-4).

A preoccupation with expensive clothes often accompanies the lust of the eyes. This is not to suggest that Christians are worldly if they are physically attractive. Yet we should realize that external eye-pleasing things are not an end in themselves. They must not rob us of an unseen inner beauty that will never be unfashionable or outdated.

(3) Pride of Life. The phrase, "the boasting of what he has and does," presents a picture of a puffed up, conceited character who insists on impressing you with his accumulation of wealth and personal accomplishments. He is a braggart who bores his listeners with self-centered descriptions of how the world could not get along without him.

Jim is thirty-one years old and works for an investment company. He is a corporate climber and leaves for his office each morning at 6:00. He often does not get home until 9:30 P.M.—long after the children have been shuttled off to bed. Jim isn't working these long hours simply to pay his bills. He's doing it because he wants to impress his friends with how successful he is. He goes out of his way to state how important he is to the company, and how he intends to be its president within the next five years. His spiritual life, however, is suffering; his family relations are in need of repair. But these matters are not as important to Jim as the great impression he wants to make on others.

Mary is in a somewhat similar situation. She speaks incessantly of her children's academic achievements. The entire neighborhood has to know that they both will be graduating at the top of their classes. She talks endlessly of how well her husband has done in his firm and reminds her church friends of the great success of her recent dinner party. If you accused Mary of being worldly she would look at you with a puzzled expression. But she has been exhibiting one of the classic symptoms of worldliness—boasting of what she has and does. Both Mary and Jim live in a manner which mirrors the non-Christian society around them. Making an impression on others is more important to them than living a holy life.

The World and Its Condemnation (2:17)

I waited impatiently at the railroad crossing as a blur of color streaked past. An Amtrak train was racing to its destination. It was there for a moment, then gone for good.

John describes the world in similar terms: "The world and its desires pass away" (v. 17). This world is in the process of passing by. The glitter and color that seems so attractive now will someday be gone. This is another reason why Christians should not love the world.

Suppose I have an opportunity to make an investment that would double my savings overnight. I am guaranteed that if I invest $5,000 in a particular company this week, I will make $10,000 next week. There's only one condition. I have to leave my money invested for two months. I would be foolish not to make this investment—unless I knew beforehand that the company was going bankrupt tomorrow. It would be *more* foolhardy for me to invest all my money in a business I knew was going broke!

The world we live in is a lot like that. I can enjoy its pleasures while it lasts. But eventually, it *will* go bankrupt—and I'll have invested the only life I have in something that is gone forever.

This is why doing the will of God is so important. It is an investment in eternity. My service for Christ and a life lived for Him pay dividends that last forever.

1 John 2:18-27

¹⁸Dear children, this is the last hour; and as you have heard that the antichrist is coming, even now many antichrists have come. This is how we know it is the last hour. ¹⁹They went out from us, but they did not really belong to us. For if they had belonged to us, they would have remained with us; but their going showed that none of them belonged to us. ²⁰But you have an anointing from the Holy One, and all of you know the truth. ²¹I do not write to you because you do not know the truth, but because you do know it and because no lie comes from the truth. ²²Who is the liar? It is the man who denies that Jesus is the Christ. Such a man is the antichrist—he denies the Father and the Son. ²³No one who denies the Son has the Father; whoever acknowledges the Son has the Father also. ²⁴See that what you have heard from the beginning remains in you. If it does, you also will remain in the Son and in the Father. ²⁵And this is what He promised us—even eternal life. ²⁶I am writing these things to you about those who are trying to lead you astray. ²⁷As for you, the anointing you received from Him remains in you, and you do not need anyone to teach you. But as His anointing teaches you about all things and as that anointing is real, not counterfeit—just as it has taught you, remain in Him.

6 The Importance
of Believing
Correctly

He sat on the sofa in our living room with his head in his hands, describing a problem that had plagued him for the last twenty years. Hal was an entrenched alcoholic—and it was destroying both him and his family. I asked him whether he ever had given his heart to Christ. "No, not really," he whispered. A few moments later, we knelt on the floor and Hal asked Christ to be the Lord of his life.

I was naive enough to think that Hal's problems were over. Actually, they were just beginning. Yet it was *not* alcohol that impeded Hal's spiritual growth. It was false teaching.

As I arrived to visit Hal a few months later, I saw two men in black suits and narrow ties leaving his house. I noticed they were carrying Bibles, so I asked Hal who they were. It turned out that a local cult recently had learned of Hal's new interest in religion. I warned him of the dangers of listening to their teaching, but as the months went by, Hal's involvement with them increased.

I would like to tell you that this story had a happy ending; unfortunately, it did not. Hal became an active member of the cult. I was learning firsthand the damaging effects that false doctrine can have on God's family. I was learning that division *within* the body of Christ—divisions that prevent us from being effective witnesses *outside* the church—often are the direct result of the insidious influence of wrong beliefs about God.

John previously outlined the problems of wrong behavior (2:15-17). He showed us that we are not to love the world or anything in it. Now the Apostle moves on to the problems of wrong belief.

John personally witnessed the destructive results of false teaching in his own day. A small group of false teachers led many Christians astray. This group brought disunity to the church and disaster to individual lives. In this epistle, John confronts the problems of wrong belief in a twofold way. First, he exposes the teachers for who they are by describing some of their traits. Then, he lists certain provisions available to every Christian—provisions that can make us more stable and less likely to yield to the pressure of new religious trends.

Identifying Spiritual Counterfeits (2:18-23)

At the close of 1 John 2 we are told that Christians need to be able to tell the difference between truth and falsehood. "His anointing teaches you about all things and as that anointing is real, not counterfeit—just as it has taught you, remain in Him (v. 27).

The ability to identify a counterfeit usually requires highly developed powers of observation. The jeweler who appraises a diamond ring, the art dealer who looks at a painting to determine whether it is a genuine Picasso, the government official who determines whether a twenty-dollar bill is the real thing—all these people have a keen eye for detail. They know, for instance, that a good counterfeit product will resemble the real commodity as closely as possible. An experienced forger always uses the correct type of paper and ink. A phony painting always attempts to match the original artist's style.

This is a point to remember when we deal with spiritual realities. Christianity, offers peace and promises a sense of security. It has high demands and requires a total commitment. It holds out a sense of belonging and unconditional love. Anyone who has studied cults knows that false sects advertise precisely these benefits. Cults are able to simulate some of the by-products of biblical Christianity, and a spiritually hungry society reaches out uncritically to embrace them.

A person who detects counterfeits also knows that in spite of surface similarities, certain features always distinguish counterfeits from the genuine item. Knowing what these traits are, and where to look for them, makes one an expert in this field. Persons skilled in detecting counterfeit currency, for example, know how to look for the tiny colored threads that are sown into all authentic U.S. paper money.

In distinguishing spiritual truths from error, it is equally important to know the characteristics of false doctrine. John gives us a number of clues in verses 18-23 to help us function as good spiritual detectives. Though these clues relate to the false teachers of John's time, they have relevant applications for us today.

They Are Increasing Numerically. John labels these false teachers "antichrists" and notes their numerical strength (v. 18). Regrettably, their numbers have not shrunk in the intervening centuries. If any-thing, the zeal of these teachers is greater today than ever; such groups continue to proliferate. They visit homes in suburbia, trying to disseminate their litera-ture and erroneous beliefs amongst an unsuspecting and biblically illiterate public. We sometimes catch sight of them moving through airports. We hear their voices on radio stations late at night, or on TV sets on Sunday morning. Their technique is polished but their message is spiritually dangerous. That is why John warns us to be spiritually alert and to evaluate carefully what we hear.

Their large numbers, moreover, are a sign of the end times. "You have heard that the antichrist is coming," John writes (v. 18). By stating this, the author reminds us that a prophetic figure of the end times will exhibit extensive power and deceive many. Paul alludes to this figure as "The man of lawlessness . . . the man doomed to destruction. He opposes and exalts himself over everything that is called God or is worshiped" (2 Thes. 2:3-4). He also is portrayed as a ferocious beast who blasphemes God, receives worship, and persecutes true believers (Rev. 13:1-8). John tells us, however, that we do not have to wait until the end of history for such a figure to arise. The coming Antichrist is preceded by con-temporary antichrists. Between now and the end of time, "little antichrists" will oppose God and lead people astray.

The presence of the predecessors of the Antichrist is a sign that "This is the last hour" (1 John 2:18). This is a puzzling statement, given the fact that nine-teen centuries have elapsed since it was made. Did John believe the end of the world was just around the corner? If so, he was hopelessly in error. The solution to this apparent problem lies in a correct understanding of the meaning of such phrases as "the last hour" or "the last days."

My son Mike was sprawled on the floor watching a hockey game when I came into the room. "How much more time is there to play?" I asked, noting that the score was tied. "It's the last period," he said, without taking his eyes off the action. At that point, I was not certain whether the period had just started, or whether the final whistle was about to blow. There could have been a lot of action still to take place, or just a few seconds before the clock ran out.

We are now in the final time period before God brings all human history to a close. We, like John, are not certain whether there is a lot of time to go or whether the end is at hand. But we *do* know this last hour may conclude at any time. We must be ready.

They May Belong to the Professing Church. Believers always have faced doctrinal threats from other world religions. But the problems described in 1 John did not result from attacks *outside* the church, but from false teachers *within* the body. These individuals professed to be believers, but did not teach fundamental Christian truths.

Present threats to Christianity can arise in a similar way. They can come from those who have teaching offices within the church. They can come from seminaries and training schools where the Scriptures are not considered authoritative. They may involve ministers who give lip service to orthodox Christian creeds and doctrinal statements, but in practice deny such statements or invest them with entirely new meanings. Error also can be spread by lay people who are not firmly grounded in biblical knowledge. They can be exposed to false doctrinal teaching without even realizing the full implications of their errors.

A secretary typing an annual report for a large corporation may make a mistake in recording a column of figures for the profit/loss statement. If her error goes undetected, it will be reproduced and distributed among hundreds of shareholders. Even though the secretary's error was not done deliberately, it will be multiplied many times over and great confusion will result. For a similar reason, Christians need carefully to examine the Gospel being preached in their churches. The teaching they share must be accurate.

John mentions that, though the false teachers had been with the group, "they did not really belong to us" (v. 19). This is a reminder that the organized, visible church is never quite as pure as we think. Despite our best efforts, nonbelievers will likely be present with believers. And if these unbelievers are active in spreading their views, serious factional problems can develop. As a result, the body of believers will be weakened. This makes the identification of spiritual counterfeits all the more important.

They Misinterpret the Person of Christ. The actual teaching of the heretics contained two fatal flaws. They denied that Jesus is the Christ, and they denied the Father and the Son (v. 22). When John says Jesus is the Christ, he uses this term to explain that Jesus is divine. Therefore, the person who denies that Jesus of Nazareth is the full embodiment of God denies the Father as well. To claim direct access to God the Father apart from God the Son is to negate the Christian message. In John's Gospel, the words of Jesus, Himself, teach the same truth: "I am the way and the truth and the life. No one comes to the Father except through Me" (John 14:6).

During the famous battle of Waterloo, a strategic plot of ground changed hands several times. Both

Napoleon and Wellington realized that whoever could take—and hold—that position, would ultimately be the victor. Wellington tenaciously clung to the position and won the fight. That one piece of ground was worth fighting for; to have relinquished it would have meant losing everything.

The truth of Christ's full deity and His unique relationship with the Father also are positions worth fighting for. If we lose these truths, we ultimately lose all that is unique to the Christian faith. We may not agree on forms of worship or the manner in which to conduct the Lord's Supper. That's alright. There is room for differences of opinion in non-essentials. But the truth in this passage is foundational. John wants us to know that it must never be surrendered.

This warning may seem so obvious that it does not even merit mentioning. After all, you've probably been a Christian for years and know the Bible thoroughly. But note what John says here: "I do not write to you because you do not know the truth, but because you do know it" (1 John 2:21). A warning always is appropriate no matter how strong we are in the faith. John isn't saying that the whole Christian community will fall into false belief; but it *is* important to be on the alert.

Appropriating God's Provision (2:20-27)

The danger described in verses 18-23 may seem alarming. John has shown us the perils of false teaching and how easy it is for even mature Christians to succumb to them. If that's the case, why bother going on? What hope can Christians have against Satan?

I once talked with a recently married Christian couple who had decided not to have any children.

"There are too many temptations and snares," they explained. "We're afraid of what would happen to our kids if we raised them in this kind of world."

I told them I thought their concern was well-founded. But at the same time, I pointed out that if they observed certain safeguards they *could* successfully raise their children for God. God in His sovereignty can overrule any evil influence and provide Christian parents with the resources necessary for overcoming Satan.

In the same way, God's power can keep all members of His family safe. Doctrinal evils are real, and new *or* older Christians may be deceived. Nevertheless, God has provided resources to guard against spiritual deception. And what are these resources? Let's add them up.

The Person of the Holy Spirit

Twice in this chapter John speaks of an "anointing" that all believers possess: "You have an anointing from the Holy One" (v. 20); "The anointing you received from Him remains in you" (v. 27). The anointing all believers have received is the Holy Spirit.

The Gospels speak of Christ being anointed with the Holy Spirit. One Saturday morning, Jesus went to the synagogue service and participated by reading the Scripture. The reading was from Isaiah, and Jesus began by announcing, "The Spirit of the Lord is upon Me, because He has anointed Me to preach" (Luke 4:18). Jesus claimed He was the fulfillment of that prophecy; as such, He was anointed by the presence of the Holy Spirit. This same anointing belongs to us as well.

Why are we anointed by His Spirit? So that we can learn. "His anointing teaches you about all things"

(1 John 2:27). In a section of John's epistle which deals with false teachers, it's appropriate to be reminded that all Christians have the true Teacher, the Holy Spirit, residing within them. Jesus Himself promised this ministry of the Spirit: "The Holy Spirit, whom the Father will send in My name, will teach you all things" (John 14:26).

I have been privileged to attend classes taught by some great Bible teachers. All had a firm grasp of God's Word and were able to relate it to daily life. But not all believers have had such opportunities. Some live in areas where good Bible teaching isn't available. Bible conferences are held many miles away and can be attended only at great personal inconvenience and cost. Yet *all* believers have constant access to the greatest Bible Teacher—the Holy Spirit. He is able to communicate God's truth—the Bible—and show us how to use it in daily life. And why shouldn't He? He is the divine Author of Scripture!

This point obviously raises a question. If the Holy Spirit's teaching is available to us all, why doesn't He reveal the same truth to each of us? Shouldn't we all possess the same understanding of the Word and believe the same thing? As things stand, Christians do *not* agree on the interpretation of every verse of the Bible. We have a variety of opinions that separate us both denominationally and doctrinally. Are we to conclude from this that the Holy Spirit is not a good teacher?

This matter of Christians believing different things used to bother me considerably. How could this be if the Spirit teaches us all? It finally occurred to me—after working for several years as a professor—that no one absorbs *everything* a teacher says. Even the best of teachers find themselves facing classroom distractions, sleepy students, and built-in prejudices against the subject matter being taught. Students inevitably fail to take in all that the teacher is giving out.

What is true on the human level is, unfortunately, also true on the spiritual plane. The Holy Spirit instructs us but Satan distracts us. We too have biases and preconceived ideas we are unwilling to relinquish. We must face the fact that we are human and imperfect. So if we disagree with one another over doctrine, it is not the fault of the divine Teacher. The problem rests with us, His human students.

Because we have the Holy Spirit, John makes two all-embracing statements: "All of you know the truth" (1 John 2:20), and "You do not need anyone to teach you" (v. 27). These verses mean that the teaching ministry of the Spirit is available to all Christians—not just a chosen few. In writing this, John is not suggesting that human teachers are unnecessary. If that were true, John himself would be unqualified to write this epistle. Yet these verses do suggest that no human teacher can be considered the ultimate authority on spiritual matters. God uses human teachers to convey His truths to others. But only the Holy Spirit is an infallible guide. The more closely we are related to Him, the more clearly we can hear His voice and respond to it.

Instruction in the Word

Any time a Christian feels the Spirit is instructing him to take a certain course of action, he must make sure this "prompting" does not contradict an external standard. And what standard should he use? The Scriptures, themselves. This is why John writes, "See that what you have heard from the beginning remains in you" (v. 24). People sometimes take foolish steps and then claim the Spirit led them to do so. Christians divorce their spouses, abandon their children, and engage in shady business practices. Their rationale for these actions? "I was led by the Spirit." But the teaching of the Spirit never contradicts the Word, and so we must constantly return to the written authority and let it remain in us. If we do not, we will float in a sea of spiritual subjectivity.

Verses 24-25 give us one of the most vital safeguards against falling into error: we are to have a thorough knowledge of basic Christian truth. It has been said that the best way to spot a counterfeit bill is to be familiar with the distinguishing features of a real one. The better a person knows the true commodity, the easier it is to identify a forgery. The same applies to Christian truth.

Some Christians believe we should study cults and have a thorough knowledge of what each one believes. There is some truth to this; but the best way to detect error is to know God's Word. This is one factor that made the early church so strong. As Luke points out, "They devoted themselves to the apostles' teaching" (Acts 2:42). It was this vital teaching that created honesty in their interpersonal relationships, spontaneity in their worship, and consistency in their evangelism. It will do the same for us.

A Healthy Relationship with Christ

The final command in this section supplies another piece of armor to use in our battle against error. We must "Remain in Him" (1 John 2:27). We already have been reminded to remain in the Son and in the Father (v. 24). The concept of remaining or abiding is an important one in 1 John. The word "remain" or "abide" appears twenty-three times in this epistle. It most often is used to describe the believer abiding or remaining in Christ—and this connotes a healthy growing relationship with Him. Growing Christians are less likely to fall into error than disgruntled ones.

John supplies the best explanation of what it means to remain in Christ in his Gospel:

> Remain in Me, and I will remain in you. No branch can bear fruit by itself; it must remain in the vine. Neither can you bear fruit unless you remain in Me. I am the vine; you are the branches. If a man remains in Me and I in him, he will bear much fruit; apart from Me you can do nothing (John 15:4-5).

To remain in Christ is to draw our life and nourishment from Him as a branch receives its life from the vine. As the vine is pruned and dead wood cut away, the fruit grows. In the same way, our relationship with Christ must be vital and productive. There is less likelihood of doctrinal dry rot weakening a Christian who is strong and healthy.

Once again, John has blended the two concepts of right belief and right behavior. They cannot be separated; one balances the other. In a day and age when cults proliferate and anti-biblical ideas run wild, a knowledge of these facts is crucial. We *must* be on guard. God has provided us with built-in safety measures to defeat false teachers. If we make use of them, we can eliminate a major source of divisiveness in God's family.

1 John 2:28—3:10

²⁸And now, dear children, continue in Him, so that when He appears we may be confident and un-ashamed before Him at His coming. ²⁹If you know that He is righteous, you know that everyone who does what is right has been born of Him. ¹How great is the love the Father has lavished on us, that we should be called children of God! And that is what we are! The reason the world does not know us is that it did not know Him. ²Dear friends, now we are children of God, and what we will be has not yet been made known. But we know that when He appears, we shall be like Him, for we shall see Him as He is. ³Everyone who has this hope in him purifies himself, just as He is pure. ⁴Everyone who sins breaks the law; in fact, sin is lawlessness. ⁵But you know that He appeared so that He might take away our sins. And in Him is no sin. ⁶No one who lives in Him keeps on sinning. No one who continues to sin has either seen Him or known Him. ⁷Dear children, do not let anyone lead you astray. He who does what is right is righteous, just as He is righteous. ⁸He who does what is sinful is of the devil, because the devil has been sinning from the beginning. The reason the Son of God appeared was to destroy the devil's work. ⁹No one who is born of God will continue to sin, because God's seed remains in him; he cannot go on sinning, because he has been born of God. ¹⁰This is how we know who the children of God are and who the children of the devil are: Anyone who does not do what is right is not a child of God; neither is anyone who does not love his brother.

7 If You Were Arrested for Being a Christian

Imagine, if you will, the following. In the country in which you now live, it is a crime to be a Christian. Government agents are assigned to monitor your every move. You are watched as you wheel your grocery cart through the aisles of the supermarket and are photographed when you approach the check-out counter. The agents note whether you tell the cashier she's given you too much change. You are under surveillance in your home. Tape recordings are made of your conversations with your family. Your church activities are videotaped for replay at a later date.

After two weeks of observation, the agents make their report. Your file is studied carefully for incriminating evidence. Is there enough data to indict you for being a Christian? Or will the case be dismissed for lack of evidence?

First John 2:28—3:10 explains that if our faith is important to us, the evidence for our Christianity will be obvious. John puts it this way: "This is how we know who the children of God are and who the children of the devil are: Anyone who does not do what is right is not a child of God; neither is anyone who does not love his brother" (3:10). There are only two families: God's and the devil's. If we are Christians, the family resemblance between us and our Father ought to be evident. In this epistle, John states that family members will exhibit this resemblance by doing what is right and by loving one another. This first trait—"doing what is right"—is developed in 2:28—3:9, and will be discussed presently. The concept of "loving one another" is explained more fully in 3:10-24, and so will be studied in the next chapter.

Doing Right

Many years ago I had a part-time job with an organization that specialized in treating severely handicapped children. Boys and girls with twisted limbs came to the Treatment Center from hundreds of miles away. One of my weekly tasks was to go to the airport or train station to meet parents who were arriving to visit their children. Though I knew the children well, in most cases I had never met their parents. I would fervently scan the faces of people coming off the train, looking for Mrs. Brown or Mr. Jones. When a family resemblance was unmistakable, I would go up and introduce myself. On other occasions, if I couldn't immediately distinguish a resemblance between family members, it would take me three or four attempts before I finally located the right person.

God has called us to be His sons and daughters; consequently, He wants our family resemblance to be clear. As we noted earlier, one family trait we are to possess involves doing what is right. This fact is repeated several times in 1 John. "Everyone who does what is right has been born of Him" (2:24); "He who does what is right is righteous" (3:7); "Anyone who does not do what is right is not a child of God" (3:10).

And what is our motivation for living a righteous life? John lists two reasons: Christ's first coming and His second coming. Note the statements the Apostle makes about the appearances of Christ:

- Continue in Him, so that when He appears we may be confident (2:28)
- When He appears, we shall be like Him (3:2)
- He appeared so that He might take away our sins (3:5)
- The reason the Son of God appeared was to destroy the devil's work (3:8)

If you study these four statements you will note that the first two relate to the future and describe Christ's return to earth. The latter two describe the past and explain why Christ initially came. Let's examine these areas more closely.

The Impact of the Second Coming (2:28—3:3)

Two years ago, our only daughter was married. Having officiated at numerous weddings myself, I assumed it would be relatively easy to make our own daughter's nuptial arrangements. Little did I realize the difference between conducting a wedding, and being actively involved in the planning for one. We had to prepare guest lists and mail out invitations. Members of the wedding party had to be chosen. Flowers and dresses needed to be purchased. A thousand details required our attention.

Our daily routines were altered for months because of the preparations for this joyous occasion. The reality of a future event affected how we lived in the present.

Christ's return also is a future event, and it too must make a difference in how we live in the present. The Second Coming is not a meaningless doctrine or a point of eschatology that has no real impact on our lives. On the contrary, the knowledge that He will be coming back should affect us in several ways.

It Builds Confidence (v. 28). If we are living a life of righteousness, we will be confident and unashamed when Christ appears. The homemaker who has just cleaned a house from top to bottom will not be embarrassed if unexpected guests drop in. A business executive who has prepared his income tax return with honesty and integrity will not be intimidated if the IRS unexpectedly audits him. A student who has prepared his class presentation thoroughly will be more confident when his turn comes to speak. Christians who seek to obey and please God will be sure of themselves as they anticipate Christ's return.

It Reflects the New Birth (v. 29). A life lived in anticipation of the Second Coming also is an indication that a person has received the new birth. As John explains, "Everyone who does what is right has been born of Him."

At first glance, it may seem as though the Apostle has things reversed here. Doesn't the new birth lead to righteous living, rather than the other way around? Actually, this verse isn't trying to explain *how* a person is born of God; rather, it's describing how to *identify* one who is born of God. It's picturing the type of person who eagerly awaits His return.

I once attended a gathering of missionary personnel in the Philadelphia area. One of the staff informed me that two French citizens who were working with North American missionaries in France would be at the meeting. I looked forward to meeting them and trying out my high school French. "You won't have any trouble finding them," the staffer said. "They'll be the only ones speaking a foreign language."

This staff member wasn't trying to tell me how these two men had come to learn their language; he simply was telling me how to recognize them in a crowd.

Christians are born of God through the Holy Spirit. But we can be *identified* because we do what is right. At Christ's return, those who have been living righteously will be easily identified.

It Reveals Our Sonship (v. 2a). This mention of the new birth now leads us to a discussion of what it means to be a member of God's family.

At the Second Coming, the family likeness between God and His children will be complete. We will see Christ and be like Him. But we need not wait until the Lord's return to enjoy our sonship. Some benefits are ours immediately. They can affect our lives in the here and now.

We can, for example, enjoy the treasures of God's matchless and unconditional love—in spite of the fact that He knows our past sins and is aware of the ways we will fail Him in the future. He is aware of the enormity of our transgressions and the flaws in our character. Yet He still reaches down, rescues us, and gives us status as members of His family.

A young lady dropped by my office one day to share something she recently had discovered in her Christian life. "I've just learned," she explained, "that God loves me with no strings attached."

"How long have you been a Christian?" I asked.

"About ten years," she replied. "Oh, I could quote John 3:16 and I knew that love is one of the attributes of God," she continued, "but I hadn't experienced it personally."

She went on to share some of the difficulties of her childhood. Starved for affection, she had turned to illicit sexual liaisons, desperately trying to find love and caring. But all she experienced was hurt. Because she bore these emotional scars, she found it difficult to open herself up to anyone's love, including God's. To be able to do that was a great step forward for her.

Fortunately, this is a step we all can take. We all are sons and daughters in the family. God's love is our inheritance.

Another truth about our sonship relates to the certainty and timelessness of our relationship with God. We are called sons of God, and that is what we are. We will be so in the present, as well as at the Second Coming.

A student takes an entrance exam, hoping to get into the university of his choice. The test has stretched his intellectual ability to the limit and he is not certain he has made the grade. Several anxious weeks pass before the results are in. He's made it!

God, on the other hand, does not make us wait in anxiety and uncertainty. He wants us to know where we stand—right now! If we have experienced the new birth we have been accepted into the family. There is no probationary period. We have full status as sons in the family because God has surrounded us with His unconditional love. We can await His return with confidence!

It Produces Purity (3:3). For Christians, the Second Coming is not intended to be a frightening prospect. John describes it as a hope, which suggests among other things, that it should give us an optimistic outlook concerning the future. It is not to be a distant reality, but a daily incentive to live a life of purity.

The details of the Lord's return hold great fascination for many people. We attend prophetic conferences and chart eschatological events. Great debates rage over who the Antichrist will be. The political situation during the Great Tribulation is carefully studied. Some Christians become downright obsessed with this topic. I'm not suggesting that such details are unimportant. But by burying ourselves in a mountain of details, we can lose the life-purifying aspects of the Second Coming.

Suppose I am planning to take a trip and tell my wife that I would like her to meet me on my return. Before I leave, I give her the airline timetable that describes my flight and when I will be arriving. Finally, after a long trip, I arrive back at the airport— but find no one there to meet me! I phone my wife, who confesses she has completely forgotten about my return. She immediately hops in the car and comes over to get me.

On the way home, Helen explains that she forgot about me because she was busy studying the airline timetable. She had become fascinated with its details and spent the last several days pouring over the routes the airlines traveled, the type of equipment they used, and the meals they served. She was so caught up with these details she forgot I was returning.

I'm quite certain no one has ever become that engrossed with an airline timetable. But we can fall into a similar trap on the spiritual level if we do not keep the practical dimension of our Lord's return before us. The Second Coming is designed to promote holiness. It must make a difference in all we do. If we live in anticipation of His return, our behavior will be pure.

The Importance of the First Coming (3:4-9)

We now move from the future to the past. If we understand the significance of Christ's first coming and His death, it too will be a deterrent to sin and a stimulus for us to do what is right. John's two statements about the appearance of Christ (vv. 5, 8) clearly explain why Christ came and why it should make a difference to us.

He Came to Deal with Our Sins (vv. 4-6). The more thoroughly we understand sin and what it does, the more effectively we can exhibit the family trait of righteousness.

Last night as I picked up the newspaper, I noticed a front-page story about a manufacturing plant a few miles from where we live. A number of workers in the plant had been exposed to dangerously high levels of airborne toxins. Officials originally had stated that this problem presented no danger to the employees' health. Later tests proved, however, that this initial assessment was wrong. The level of poisonous chemicals in the air exceeded the safety level by seven times. Hundreds of workers had been exposed over a period of time without realizing the danger they were in.

Sin operates in muchs the same fashion. It has an insidious effect on the believer's life. It can spiritually weaken and poison him without his even realizing it. We need, therefore, to recognize certain facts about sin.

(1) Sin is a disregard for God's law (v. 4). Theologians have defined sin in a variety of ways. Some see it merely as the behavior of a poorly adjusted person.

It is a personality flaw that easily can be remedied if the individual so desires. Others define sin as selfishness and self-centeredness. This is partly true, but hardly the whole story.

John describes a sinner as one who breaks God's law, and defines sin as lawlessness or rebellion. These explanations capture the essence of sin because they view sin in relation to God. Sin is a repudiation of God's laws and thus insults His holy and sovereign character. While we can describe sin in terms of its effect on our personalities, thoughts, and acts, we also must recognize it as an affront to God. By breaking the law, criminals demonstrate their lack of respect for the authorities who formulate and enforce those laws. A failure to observe God's laws is a similar expression of rebellion.

(2) Sin is a repudiation of Christ's work (v. 5). The primary purpose of Christ's coming to earth was to deal with the rebellion and lawlessness of which we have been speaking. Christ endured a criminal's death with all its disgrace and shame. He experienced the hell of separation from God so that we might be released from the sin that binds us. If I continue to live in sin, my life is a contradiction of this eternal work of Christ. I am then working at cross-purposes with God since He sent His Son to deal decisively with sin.

(3) Sin is a contradiction of the Christian's testimony (v. 6). In this verse, John makes two statements concerning the believer and sin that have puzzled many Bible students. Do these statements indicate that if a person sins, he cannot be a true believer? Similarly, does verse 9 mean that the one born of God is incapable of sin? One obvious difficulty with such interpretations is that they contradict what John already has told us: namely, if we claim to

be without sin we are fooling ourselves (1:8).

Perhaps John is speaking only of certain *types* of sin. Or perhaps he means that real Christians do not sin deliberately—only accidentally. Others have suggested that this verse means real Christians do not sin in their actions, only in their thoughts. Once again, these analyses must be rejected. Nowhere does the passage make distinctions of this sort.

A more realistic possibility is that John is giving an admonition in the form of a statement. When he states that Christians *do* not sin, he really means Christians *should* not sin.

As I arrived home one evening, I heard Helen lecturing one of our sons. A delicious dessert that had been sitting on the kitchen counter was now missing. Our son initially claimed he knew nothing about it; later, he changed his story and admitted he had devoured the dessert a short time before dinner.

"Good boys don't tell lies," my wife admonished him. That was an interesting choice of words. Though Helen expressed her feelings in the form of a statement, she obviously intended them to be understood as a command: "Don't lie!"

In the same way, the statements of verse 6 can mean, "Do not sin if you are a Christian." That's a command, even though John puts his words in the form of a descriptive statement.

Another possible explanation of this passage: Christians do not sin *continuously.* This thought is captured in the words, "No one who lives in Him *keeps on* sinning. No one who *continues* to sin has either seen Him or knows Him" (v. 6; italics mine). In other words, although individual acts of sin may arise in a Christian's life, they do not mark his behavior as a distinguishing characteristic.

Two weeks ago, a friend told me he found it

relaxing to play a weekly game of golf. He asked me if I enjoyed the sport. "No," I replied. "I don't play golf." Actually, he could have challenged my statement. I *have* played golf on occasion. But my last outing produced sore feet, a painful sunburn, and a score of 179 for the eighteen holes. I realized my friend was talking about golf as a habitual, ongoing pursuit—so I replied accordingly.

This interpretation of verse 6 probably fits best with the context of John's overall message. He does not want members of God's family to sin habitually or with impunity. If we do, this passage challenges the reality of our faith. It shows us that we must not allow sin to get out of control.

He Came to Destroy the Devil (vv. 7-9). In this passage we are reminded that sin is the devil's business. From the very beginning, rebellion against God has characterized Satan's mission. That is why Christ came—to destroy the devil and his works. Therefore, if I sin, I am at cross-purposes with the coming of Christ; furthermore, I am aiding the devil and his cause.

When Satan comes calling, it's good to remember that he no longer has any authority over us. As the author of Hebrews notes in writing of the death of Christ, "He too shared in their humanity so that by His death He might destroy him who holds the power of death—that is, the devil—and free those who all their lives were held in slavery" (Hebrews 2:14-15).

As an office manager for a large insurance company, Bill supervises 250 typists and stenographers. For years, he has made unreasonable demands on his workers and treated them like slaves. He barks out orders and is impossible to please. His employees live in fear of his presence and avoid him whenever possible. One Wednesday afternoon, word leaks out that Bill's been fired. The company's been getting a lot of comlaints about him, so he's being relieved of his responsibilities. Though this order is effective immediately, Bill is allowed to stay until the end of the week to clean out his desk.

Even though he's been fired, Bill continues to follow his normal patterns. He keeps on issuing his nasty orders and acting like a big shot. The office staff, surprisingly, continues to obey him. After all, they've been doing so for years. Obviously, someone needs to remind these workers that Bill's authority is gone. He no longer has the right to order them around. They need to resist his demands! It's just a matter of time until he's gone for good!

The believer lives in a similar situation in relation to Satan. The devil's power is gone. Christ's sacrifice on the cross has released us from him and his sinful works. We simply must learn to resist him. It is only a matter of time until the sentence passed at Calvary will be carried out completely and Satan will be gone for good.

Think of a situation where you are tempted to do what is wrong. Someone is encouraging you to complain about your pastor or to start a splinter group in your church. Or perhaps you're tempted to treat another member of God's family in a hostile way. Now think of Christ's first coming and the purpose for which He came. Think about His second coming and what that will mean for you. Then ask God for the strength to do what is right. Only then can God's family enjoy freedom from the influence of Satan. Only then can we live in an atmosphere of loving servanthood with one another.

1 John 3:10-24

[10]This is how we know who the children of God are and who the children of the devil are: Anyone who does not do what is right is not a child of God; neither is anyone who does not love his brother. [11]This is the message you heard from the beginning: We should love one another. [12]Do not be like Cain, who belonged to the evil one and murdered his brother. And why did he murder him? Because his own actions were evil and his brother's were righteous. [13]Do not be surprised, my brothers, if the world hates you. [14]We know that we have passed from death to life, because we love our brothers. Anyone who does not love remains in death. [15]Anyone who hates his brother is a murderer, and you know that no murderer has eternal life in him. [16]This is how we know what love is: Jesus Christ laid down His life for us. And we ought to lay down our lives for our brothers. [17]If anyone has material possessions and sees his brother in need but has no pity on him, how can the love of God be in him? [18]Dear children, let us not love with words or tongue but with actions and in truth. [19]This then is how we know that we belong to the truth, and how we set our hearts at rest in His presence [20]whenever our hearts condemn us. For God is greater than our hearts, and He knows everything. [21]Dear friends, if our hearts do not condemn us, we have confidence before God [22]and receive from Him anything we ask, because we obey His commands and do what pleases Him. [23]And this is His command: to believe in the name of His Son, Jesus Christ, and to love one another as He commanded us. [24]Those who obey His commands live in Him, and He in them. And this is how we know that He lives in us: We know it by the Spirit He gave us.

8 Things Go Better
with Love

As I made my way to the cash register at the book store last Saturday, I noticed the Romance Section was stocked with new releases. *Why do people keep buying these fantasies?* I asked myself as I plucked a paperback out of the rack. The summary on the back cover contained few surprises. Poor, deprived, yet beautiful young girl falls in love with handsome young man. Little does she realize when they meet at an opulent villa on a South Pacific island that he actually is a millionaire. Several hundred pages later, they walk off into the sunset, hand in hand, to live happily ever after.

Does the popularity of these pseudo-love stories say something about the absence of the real thing in our lives? Are people so starved for intimacy and significant relationships they'll grab anything that re-motely resembles the genuine commodity? What an opportunity for the church to fill this emotional void!

I have just one question. Are Christians responding

to this challenge? John states that as believers, we are to have compassion for other people—particularly other Christians. He underlines this mark of real faith in 3:10 and develops this characteristic throughout the remainder of chapter 3. In that chapter, the Apostle leaves no doubt: One of the traits of our sonship is our willingness to meet the challenge of love.

Nowadays, there's no scarcity of cute slogans and colorful bumper stickers heralding the magnificence of love.

Love is a many-splendored thing.
Love makes the world go round.
Love means never having to say you're sorry.

Talk is cheap and definitions of love are easy to formulate. John takes a more practical approach. He realizes the term "love" has been hopelessly overworked. So he chooses to *describe* love, rather than simply add another platitude to the collection.

In this passage, John highlights three features of biblical love: It is a proof of our sonship (3:10-15); it is patterned after the work of Christ (3:16-18); and it provides assurance (3:19-24).

Love Is a Proof of Our Sonship (3:10-15)

Verse 10 is a hinge verse in 1 John 3; it looks both backward and forward. As we noted in chapter 7, a real believer does what is right and loves his brother. We've already examined the first of these traits— doing what is right. Now let's look at the second trait of true Christianity as it's expanded in the latter part of chapter 3.

Christian Love Is Intramural. These verses say a lot about loving fellow Christians, but nothing about loving unbelievers. The use of the word "brother" in verses 10, 14, and 15 indicates that other members of God's family should be the target of our love. Why is it that John is strangely silent about loving non-Christians? Should we be indifferent about reaching out to the world? This obviously is not the case. Once again, John simply is stressing the need for love *within* the family of God as a prerequisite for effective ministry *outside* the family.

If you were to conduct an informal poll, most Christians probably would say it's easier to love fellow Christians than it is to love nonbelievers. Actually, I'm not so sure about that. I think we tend to expect *more* of fellow believers; after all, they're coheirs of Christ! Don't we tend to be more disappointed if *they* let us down?

What does this mean? Basically, members of our immediate Christian family—the church—are more prone to be the recipients of our selfishness, anger, and indifference than nonbelievers. In effect, John is telling us to "start at home" if we're interested in loving others. He knows that if we can love our fellow believers in the manner he describes, this love will overflow family boundaries and touch those outside the church.

A Tale of Two Brothers. This passage also illustrates the principles of love and hate by delving into the Old Testament and explaining the story of Cain and Abel. Both brothers tried to please God by bringing an acceptable sacrifice to Him. God was pleased with Abel's sacrifice and commended him for it. Yet when God refused Cain's gift, Cain exploded in anger. Though Cain's quarrel really was with God, he directed his hatred toward Abel. Eventually, Cain's violence and anger became so overwhelming that he murdered his brother.

This familiar incident illustrates the point John is trying to make in vv. 10-15. Here are two brothers who belong to the same *human* family, but who are members of different *spiritual* families. One is a child of God, the other a child of the devil. Cain exemplifies the meaning of 1 John 3:10; he lacks the two traits outlined in that verse. His murderous act sprang from his dual failure to do what is right and to exercise love. Cain slew Abel "Because his own actions were evil and his brother's were righteous" (v. 12).

Hatred, anger, and murder clearly are tied together. Murder is an outward act that stems from a hatred and anger which boils within. Jesus taught this very principle: "You have heard that it was said to the people long ago, 'Do not murder, and anyone who murders will be subject to judgment.' But I tell you that anyone who is angry with his brother will be subject to judgment" (Matt. 5:21-22).

This does not mean that hatred and anger are as serious in their effects as murder. But it does suggest that when hatred springs up in my heart, it is the first step on a road which ultimately could lead to that crime. A person with a case of appendicitis usually does not die. But if the diseased organ is left to fester, its poison can spread throughout the whole body. Peritonitis will develop and the results can be fatal. Hatred is the same. Spiritual surgery is called for when its symptoms first appear. If corrective steps are not taken, the poison will get the better of us, as it did with Cain.

We should follow the steps of Abel, who harbored no malice or hatred, who practiced righteousness instead of evil. Yet by following Abel's footsteps, we also can expect the same treatment he received— hatred from members of the devil's family. John pursues this very thought: "Do not be surprised, my brothers, if the world hates you" (1 John 3:13).

This hatred does not always express itself in open violence. It does not necessarily mean your neighbors will throw rocks through your windows or slash your car's tires. But you *will* feel their quiet, passive resentment. You possess an inner peace they do not. The integrity of your life exposes the dishonesty and shallowness in their own. Your life may not be threatened as Abel's was, but if you're the object of the same smoldering hatred, you should not be surprised.

Crossing the Border. In contrast to the hatred we receive from the world, we give and receive love as members of God's family. These actions prove we have passed from death to life (v. 14). The imagery used in this verse is of a person passing from one state to another, or of someone crossing the border into new territory. We formerly resided in the country of death, but we have had our exit permits stamped and now live in the kingdom of life.

As a Canadian resident, I often fly across the international border that separates Canada from the United States. From the air, it's difficult to determine exactly when I've crossed that border. But once I land in the United States, it's clear that I am in a new country. Its citizens use a different currency. The Stars and Stripes fly from the nearest flagpole. The people usually speak with a slight accent! I've no doubt that I am in a new environment.

Becoming a Christian is like crossing a border. We may not know the precise date we left the kingdom of darkness, but once we do leave it, we can have clear indications we've arrived in a new region. One such sign is that we have a new appreciation and love for God's people.

"What sort of measurable progress have you made in your life this year?" I asked my Bible study for new Christians.

"I have a greater hunger for God's Word," Beth said.

"I can talk with other people about spiritual things more naturally," Joanne responded.

"I am more honest in my business dealings," Alec stated.

"I like to be around Christians," George offered.

"A year ago I wouldn't have been seen dead in this Bible Study. Now I have a growing appreciation for the Bible and especially for other Christians," Laura confessed. The group agreed. They all felt that way. They had crossed the border!

Love Is Patterned after the Life of Christ (3:16-18)

Many people need a model to demonstrate how Christian love works in real life. That model is Christ Himself. And in studying His example of love, we're not only to focus on the way Christ *lived,* but on the way He *died.* As John puts it: "This is how we know what love is: Jesus Christ laid down His life for us" (v. 10). The character of His love can be summarized in three words. It is sacrificial (v. 16); it is simple (v. 17); and it is sincere (v. 18).

Love Is Sacrificial (v. 16). The love we exhibit is "Calvary love," and it is ours because of Christ's sacrificial death. Earlier in this chapter, John noted that Cain is best remembered for *taking* a life. Christ is known for *giving* His life. Regrettably, we live in a world where most people belong to the family of Cain. They are more concerned about what they can receive from life than what they can give. Their litany is familiar: "What's in it for me? How will doing such and such further my career? How will it make my life easier?" Such questions indicate that these people are takers, not givers. Yet this situation offers Christians a golden opportunity: we can be givers and follow the model of Christ, rather than the model of Cain.

John highlights Christ's death because it accurately displays the costly nature of divine love. Torrents of well-meaning words about love usually never get translated into costly acts. But the magnificent nature of Christ's love is seen in His departure from heaven and His sojourn on earth, His willingness to endure the limitations of a human body, His willingness to undergo the horror of a criminal's death, and most of all, His experience of abandonment by God Himself.

It's easy to strum our guitars and sing choruses about Christian love. It's more costly to become deeply involved in the lives of wounded, broken people. It may disrupt our schedule to drive someone to the hospital for a treatment. It may be emotionally draining to sit down and talk with a distraught wife or husband whose spouse recently has filed for divorce. But these sorts of actions are the hallmark of Christian love.

An acquaintance of mine conducts several Bible studies on a weekly basis. One day, he received a phone call from one of his class members. A close relative had been killed in a tragic accident. Could he stop by to comfort the family? My acquaintance explained that his day already was filled with a variety of responsibilities. He could not possibly be there.

That one decision permanently alienated him from the class member who called for help. "He didn't care enough to change his schedule," the student told me later. "He wasn't there when we needed him." Caring is costly. The death of Jesus tells us that.

Often, people are afraid to reach out in love because they've previously been taken advantage of. "I've been burned," they explain. "I won't take the risk of being used like that again." We certainly should resist being manipulated by people who try to use us for their own purposes. But we must remember that every act of sacrificial love involves some risk. However, that's part of the cost of "Calvary love."

Love Is Simple (v. 17). John's remarks in verse 16 could lead to a misunderstanding. That verse told us that Christ laid down His life for us, and we should do the same for our brothers. Does this mean we have to become modern martyrs, giving our lives in a foreign country for missionary service? Or what if there's a Communist takeover in our country? Will we hide believers in our attic and risk facing the firing squad? Such opportunities may come our way—but if they do, they will be rare.

Actually, love can be demonstrated in simple ways—such as paying our bills on time, picking up clothes around the house, or doing the dishes without being asked. This is the point of verse 17. Love can be exhibited simply by reaching out to meet a material need. And to practice this type of love, we just need to follow a few basic guidelines.

(1) Love must affect a definite object. Verse 17 literally reads, "If you see *the* brother in need." It tells us we must concern ourselves with aiding *specific* people. We can think in lofty generalities but never get down to specifics. We need constantly to check up on ourselves. Do I have a real person with a definite need to whom I am currently ministering? Is my home open to those who are considered losers in the game of life? Are my possessions, automobile, and savings account at God's disposal for such purposes?

Have I learned the truth that I can demonstrate love through my life as eloquently as I can by my death?

(2) We must focus on a demonstrable need. Verse 17 explains that part of the loving process involves our ability to see a brother in need. This suggests that I must be observant. Glaring needs may be right before my eyes, but I can be so busy looking after my own concerns that I never see them. After all, I have shopping to do and bills to pay. I'm busy acting as a family chauffeur, transporting my children to their extracurricular activities. I'm planning next summer's vacation. I *know* other people have needs. I'm just too preoccupied to do anything about them.

I chatted with an older couple one afternoon about their anxieties over their children. They were especially distressed about their married daughter. She was trapped in a marriage that had become unbearable. Her husband had lost his job and refused to take any responsibility for her and their two small children.

"I feel let down," the father told me. "They attend a church where the members pride themselves on caring for each other. But no one has come to their aid." In other words, this father was pointing out that a young couple was constrained to suffer in private because their church was not alert to their needs.

To identify a demonstrable need, though, we must be *more* than observant. We also must know how to evaluate whether a certain need is legitimate or not. It's often difficult to know whether a need is genuine or if it's a selfish desire. We must keep in mind that what a person asks for isn't always what he or she needs.

I had a visitor drop by my office one day last week. He explained his problems to me and asked if I could help him. His need—as he evaluated it—was finan-

cial. He wondered if I could provide him with some
funds and a place to live. In fact, he felt perhaps God
was leading him to come live with my wife and me!
On more than one occasion, Helen and I have invited
people to live with us because it met a need for
them. In this case, however, I explained that he
would have to take some initiative on his own. His
greatest need at that point was not free room and
board. It was to learn how to become responsible
and self-reliant. I had to turn down his request.

Sometimes, the best way to show love is to say no.
It may be easier to give a person what he or she asks
for and avoid a confrontation. Love, however, must
be tough as well as tender.

(3) I must have available resources. Verse 17 mentions having material possessions and seeing another
person lacking them. The implication here is that I
already possess what the needy party requires. However, if I am unemployed and cannot pay my own
bills, I'll have difficulty responding to someone else's
request for funds. This same principle also applies to
our possession of personal, psychological, and emotional resources.

A young lady recently saw me for counseling
about some personal problems. She had no job, no
self-worth, and considered suicide on a daily basis.
The longer we talked, the more I realized how complex her difficulties were. I thought that some sort of
anti-depressive medication might help her a bit, but I
certainly was in no position to prescribe it. What she
required at that point was something I was unable to
give, so I referred her to a Christian psychiatrist who
was better equipped to cope with her problems.

Some Christians adopt a "Messiah complex" and
feel only *they* can meet a person's needs. But soon
they've spread themselves so thin they cannot minis-

ter effectively to anyone. If we respond to every
need—real or perceived—we will find ourselves
emotionally exhausted. Even Jesus did not respond
to every request for help that came to Him. Like Him,
we must establish priorities, determine what person
or persons God would have us relate to, and decide
to what extent we can become involved with them.
Only then will we have the resources available to
cope with others.

Love Is Sincere (v. 18). In this verse John reminds
us that actions and truth are more important than
words. Verse 18 does not mean we should never
verbalize our love, it simply means we should not
stop there. In the Story of the Prodigal Son (Luke
15:21-24), the father didn't merely welcome the
prodigal back with words. He bought the son new
clothes and planned a party in his honor.

The love described in this part of 1 John places an
emphasis on actions. Actions are more important
than words when it comes to love. They're also more
important than feelings. Yet many people relate love
to feelings; that is, if they don't *feel* a burning desire
to help someone, they do nothing.

Perhaps a neighbor needs to know you're praying
for him or her. All you have to do is make a phone
call and share your concern. Instead, you decide to
wait until you *feel* more like reaching out with an
encouraging word. More than likely, you'll never
make that call. Satan will see to it that you never have
the right feelings for the task.

What should you do, then? Move into action *now,*
and let your feelings catch up with you later!

This principle can relate to any task or duty which
confronts us. We may not *feel* like tackling that sink
of dirty dishes, reviewing for a math exam, or mow-
ing the lawn. We need to act anyway. Good feelings

probably will come when the task is successfully *completed* rather than before it is *attempted.* Love is the same way. Make that hospital visit. Take dinner to a neighbor who has just moved in. Help someone clean out his garage. This is the love in "actions and in truth" of which the passage speaks.

Love Provides Assurance (3:19-24)
Many of John's readers had become unsettled in their faith and weren't sure that their relationship with Christ was genuine. One way to determine the reality of our standing with God is to see His supernatural love at work within us. This gives us confidence that our lives really have changed and our faith is authentic. This final section of chapter 3 provides us with an opportunity to analyze what happens when we *are* sure of our relationship with Christ.

The Condemning Heart (vv. 19-20). About a year after I became a Christian, I went through a period when I was attacked by doubts. I began to question whether my "decision" for Christ was real at all. I remember one time in particular when I succumbed to an attack of spiritual anxiety. I reviewed the night, twelve months before, when a pastor had explained salvation to me. *Was I really genuine when I asked Christ into my heart?* I wondered. *What about my inconsistencies in the past few months? Perhaps I am not a Christian at all.* Eventually, I worked my way through those feelings and my Christian life took a turn for the better. At the time, I didn't realize this was an all-too-common experience for new Christians. And I didn't know John had a label for it. He calls this type of feeling "the condemning heart" (vv. 19-20).

Our hearts condemn us when our emotions overpower our intellect. We respond to situations on the basis of how we *feel,* rather than by relying on what we *know.* I stood with my wife in front of a roller coaster in an amusement park in Florida. "Get on with me. It's perfectly safe. You'll enjoy yourself a lot more than you think," I pleaded convincingly. Helen didn't share my enthusiasm and rejected the offer—despite earnest entreaties from the rest of the family. She had been on a roller coaster many years before, and it was one of the most frightening experiences of her life. Consequently, her feelings now were far stronger than any logical arguments I could offer. Her feelings won the day.

When our hearts condemn us, we allow our emotions to get behind the wheel; our intellects are thrown into the backseat. When this happens, we must remember two things. The first is that "God is greater than our hearts"; the second is that "He knows everything" (v. 20). This is why we must live by what God says, and not only by how we feel.

I carefully went through the steps of the Gospel message with Eric and Cindy. They were a young couple whose hearts were prepared for salvation through the faithful witness of some friends. When I had finished talking, they both expressed an eagerness to ask Christ to be Lord of their lives. When we had finished praying, Cindy exclaimed, "I know for sure I'm a Christian now. I feel so much better!"

"Suppose you wake up next week and you don't feel as good?" I asked. "What then?"

There was a pause. She was not sure. I pointed out to her that it's natural to feel better when Christ removes our guilt and sin. At the same time, our salvation is grounded not in how we *feel,* but in what God *says.* God's Word is the real anchor for our spiritual experience.

The Confident Heart (vv. 21-24). Confidence in

our relationship with God, and an assurance that He accepts us, can help us grow in two other areas of our spiritual life. First, we learn about answered prayer; second, we develop ongoing obedience. John outlines these two areas in chapter 3: "We have confidence before God and receive from Him anything we ask because we obey His commands and do what pleases Him" (vv. 21-22).

A link exists between the effectiveness of our prayer life and the assurance we have in our relationship with God. When I was seventeen, I had just begun to enjoy the freedom that comes from using the family car on weekends. Once, however, while backing up the car, I accidently gunned it into a pile of lumber that sat near our driveway. I heard a sickening crunch as the wood shattered the tail light and put a noticeable dent in the rear fender. After returning the keys to my father and explaining what had happened, a brief, but distinct chill settled over our relationship. For days, I didn't know if I had ruined my relationship with my dad. Needless to say, with the status of our relationship in doubt, I didn't ask him for any special favors—particularly ones that pertained to the car!

Our prayer life can be affected in the same way. That is, if I'm unsure of my relationship with God, I will not feel free to make requests of Him. But if my relationship is solid and healthy, I have a freedom to come to God and ask Him for what I need.

The second area in which we can grow relates to obedience. A healthy relationship with God gives us a desire to please and obey Him. This obedience needs to be exercised particularly in the areas of fatih and love. We are to direct our faith to God—specifically, to His Son, Jesus Christ, and we are to direct our love to the family of God (v. 23). These are two of the epistle's basic commands. We can't think about moving into advanced areas of obedience if we have not mastered the fundamentals.

With this mention of love, John's argument has come full circle. There is no doubt about it. Love demonstrates the reality of our relationship with God. And costly obedience in the most practical areas of life will cement that relationship. A life lived in this fashion presents a powerful testimony to saved and unsaved alike. It can heal the divisions *within* God's family and prepare us for ministry *outside* the church. Simply stated, things do go better with love!

1 John 4:1-6

[1]Dear friends, do not believe every spirit, but test the spirits to see whether they are from God, because many false prophets have gone out into the world. [2]This is how you can recognize the Spirit of God: Every spirit that acknowledges that Jesus Christ has come in the flesh is from God, [3]but every spirit that does not acknowledge Jesus is not from God. This is the spirit of the antichrist, which you have heard is coming and even now is already in the world. [4]You, dear children, are from God and have overcome them, because the One who is in you is greater than the one who is in the world. [5]They are from the world and therefore speak from the viewpoint of the world, and the world listens to them. [6]We are from God, and whoever knows God listens to us; but whoever is not from God does not listen to us. This is how we recognize the Spirit of truth and the spirit of falsehood.

9 On Being a Good
Spiritual Detective

I love to watch reruns of the old "Columbo" TV series. In a typical episode, the ingenious detective arrives at the scene of the crime in his rusty old automobile, looking as though he has just tumbled out of bed. He paces back and forth in his rumpled tan trench coat, asking disarming—but penetrating—questions. Before long, he's ferreted out his suspect. It's only a matter of time before the guilty party is trapped in a contradiction and confesses to the murder.

Detective Colombo possessed an inner radar that enabled him to focus in on anyone who was not telling the truth. Christians need to possess this same detective instinct. We need to be able to track down error and unmask spiritual imposters. Our world is filled with people masquerading as genuine believers; their mission is to dupe unsuspecting Christians. True believers need to know, therefore, exactly who they are facing in this battle and what tactics their opposition is using. The greater our understanding of the enemy's strategy, the greater our potential for victory.

In 1 John 4:1-6, the Apostle gives his readers a warning. We must be on guard against error presenting itself in the guise of truth. We must be good spiritual detectives and know what to look for. We must not be deceived.

With these thoughts in mind, John provides us with a series of tests to determine whether we are dealing with truth, or with falsehood attractively packaged for Christian consumption. The concerns of chapter 4 are introduced at the end of chapter 3:"And this is His command: to believe in the name of His Son, Jesus Christ, and to love one another as He commanded us" (3:23).

According to this verse, God wants us to do two things: believe correctly and behave correctly. We encountered this two-part emphasis earlier in 1 John; as you will recall, these two items constitute two of the tests of genuine Christian experience. The doctrinal test—that of correct belief—is now developed further in 4:1-6. The moral test—that of brotherly love—will be expounded in 4:7-21. Like the two wings of an airplane, orthodoxy and orthopraxy keep the Christian in balance and flying straight.

Some Christians are particularly concerned with the issue of orthodoxy, or correct belief. They carefully study the doctrinal position of their church and can easily spot the slightest deviation from it. Yet if these believers do not balance their devotion to doctrine with brotherly love, they will become brittle and insensitive to those who disagree with them.

At the other extreme, we find Christians interested in cultivating personal relationships with nonbelievers at the expense of truth. They practice a spirit of acceptance, but have no foundation on which to build their beliefs. Theirs becomes merely another of the many self-help philosophies that have proliferated in our day.

Because of the importance of this issue, the epistle returns to it for a second time.

The Basic Warning (4:1)

John has told us that believing is an integral part of Christian experience (3:23). *Not* believing certain things is just as important. Note the two sides to this truth:

> And this is His command: to believe.... (3:23)
> Dear friends, do not believe.... (4:1)

These are not contradictory statements. They simply relate to different aspects of the same teaching. We are to obey the Holy Spirit, but other spirits—unholy spirits—must be identified and resisted. In short, all spiritual experience and spiritual phenomena do not have their source in God.

Spiritual Gullibility. The passages immediately preceding and following verses 4:1-6 speak of a love that is accepting and genuine. It is important for God's family to practice this type of love in their dealings with one another—but to practice it correctly. To totally accept someone does not mean we condone all of his or her actions. Christians often confuse these two concepts. We feel if we are to embrace others in Christian love, we must put our stamp of approval on all they do and say.

Actually, the correct form of behavior in this regard is found in the life of Jesus. He reached out in love and acceptance to the woman at the well. But in no way did He condone her sinful behavior; in fact,

He exposed it (John 4:16-18). Jesus told the woman caught in adultery that He did not condemn her; yet He did not approve of her life of sin (John 8:10-11).

Christians must be cautious as well as caring. A genuine love for others must not degenerate into spiritual gullibility. We must not allow our respect for others to prevent us from exposing false teaching—regardless of how attractively it is packaged.

Recently, I talked with a group of Christians about the dangers of false teaching. The name of a contemporary religious TV program came up and I indicated that an individual who appeared on the show was a false prophet. Some were astounded I would say such a thing. "But he's always quoting from the Bible," one said. "He seems to know his Bible so well," another added. I suggested that those things were not the sole test of a person's faith. There were other criteria, some of which John mentions here in 1 John, that disqualified him as a true teacher of the Word of God.

Even sincerity, important as that is, must not be the final test of correct belief. People can teach convincingly and sway others—but they may be leading their followers in the wrong direction.

Last June, our church planned to go on a picnic. It was to be held at a state park about thirty miles away. Most of us had never been there before, but on the day of the picnic, one driver said he knew the route from memory and offered to lead us. He assured us he had been to the park often and would watch in his rearview mirror to make sure we all were following him. Two hours later he pulled the caravan off to the side of the highway and admitted he was hopelessly lost. He apologized profusely for his mistake. While no one questioned his sincerity, his remorse didn't make up for our fruitless wandering.

Sincerity will not make a patient well if the doctor prescribes an incorrect dosage of drugs or uses the wrong kind of treatment. Sincere sorrow will not restore a lost fortune if an investment counselor recommends placing money in bad stocks. Neither will it undo the spiritual damage produced when a false teacher leads his flock in the wrong direction.

The Need for Testing. I was driving home from a Good Friday service when a police car pulled me over. The officer stuck his head in my window and informed me I was traveling twenty miles over the speed limit; he would have to issue me a speeding ticket.

"You're probably wondering how I caught you," he said. (I wasn't.) "I have a new detection device in my squad car," he continued. "I was traveling in the opposite direction and when I passed you, I was able to record your speed on my equipment."

When you stop to think about it, we are surrounded by detection devices. Metal detectors in airports sound an alarm if firearms are smuggled on a plane. Hidden cameras monitor customers in the neighborhood drug mart to identify shoplifters. More sophisticated methods are used to expose drug dealers.

We need similar tests to expose spiritual counterfeits. "Test the spirits," John advises. "Make certain they have God as their point of origin." A friend once told me his company had assigned him an interesting task. A competitor had illegally reproduced appliances made by my friend's firm, hoping to pawn them off on an unsuspecting public. "My boss sent me to a department store and told me to look for the imitation products. The general public might be fooled by a phony," he said, "but not me. I'll be able to tell in a minute whether the appliances came from

our factory, or whether they're cheap imitations."
One way or another, he claimed, he would shut the
counterfeiters down. It was simply a case of knowing
what to look for.

Christians need to have this same ability. We need
to be able to detect false prophets. The mere presence of "spiritual" activity does not guarantee that
God has put His mark of approval on it. Jesus issued
this very warning: "Watch out for false prophets.
They come to you in sheep's clothing, but inwardly
they are ferocious wolves" (Matt. 7:15). Christ also
explained that even the performing of miracles or
the uttering of prophecies did not guarantee they
were of God (Matt. 7:21-23). It may not be the Holy
Spirit at work, but unholy spirits who are doing these
things.

It is important, then, to be on the alert. The world
is crowded with false teaching. It is essential to
distinguish between the voice of truth and the voices
of error.

The Detailed Procedure (4:2-6)

The Apostle John has indicated our need to "test the
spirits" (1 John 4:1). He now tells us *how* to test
them and *what* to look for as we determine whether
a teacher is on the side of truth or error. Devising
such a test is not as easy as it may seem. I have been a
classroom teacher for over twenty years, but coming
up with questions for an examination still is a difficult procedure. The test may turn out to be too easy
or too hard. The questions may not be as clearly
formulated as they should be. They may be too
lengthy for the time allotted. They may not reveal
what I'm looking for.

Fortunately, John has devised a thorough, two-part
test for detecting spiritual error. One part of it might

be called a "speaking" test, since it involves assessing what a teacher says or "acknowledges" (vv. 2-3). The second part of the test could best be described as a "hearing" test, since it identifies who listens to true and false teachers (vv. 4-6).

The Speaking Test (vv. 2-3). There are two types of spirits: the Holy Spirit and unholy spirits. Accordingly, each type of spirit has a different origin: one comes from God, the other from Satan. We determine the difference between the two by observing what these spirits say or acknowledge.

The word "acknowledge" is the same term John uses when he writes about confessing our sin (1:9). To confess or acknowledge our sin means to accept God's evaluation of it. In the same way, if our spirit confesses or acknowledges "that Jesus Christ is come in the flesh," we embrace God's own explanation of who His Son is and what He has come to do. This confession is more than just a mechanical verbalizing of the truth. I can repeat the Apostles' Creed backward and forward. This does not necessarily mean I am committed to its truths in a personal way, or that I even understand it. Each morning during Vacation Bible School, our students would pledge allegiance to the flag. As I stood beside a blond-haired, six-year-old girl, I heard her solemnly affirm, "I pledge a legion to the flag of the United States of America...." This young lady was sincere, but she obviously did not understand what she was saying.

When John says we must acknowledge Jesus Christ, he means we must understand what we are saying and be personally committed to it. Paul explains this requirement well: "If you confess [acknowledge] with your mouth, 'Jesus is Lord,' and believe in your heart God raised Him from the dead, you will be saved" (Rom. 10:9-10). This outward acknowledgment is the visible sign of an inward belief.

To acknowledge that Jesus Christ has come in the flesh means we believe He had a previous existence with the Father. This confession of our spirit entails a belief in His full humanity as well as His deity. It affirms He is a Person worthy of our allegiance.

Last week I watched a noon-hour talk show. A popular writer was being interviewed and the host asked him what he thought of Jesus. "I see Jesus as one of the greatest men who ever lived," he began. "He has always been one of my heroes, right up there with Gandhi and Albert Schweitzer." He explained further, "I don't worship Him, of course. I definitely don't think Jesus was God."

This celebrity's sincerity was obvious. His message, though, reflected the spirit of antichrist. His spirit had acknowledged or confessed a falsehood. He was denying some basic truths about the Person and work of Jesus Christ. Any discriminating Christian who heard this remark would have to conclude the person who spoke it had failed "the speaking test" for correct belief.

The Hearing Test (vv. 4-6). John explains that many people in the world listen to false teachers precisely because these teachers speak from the *viewpoint* of the world (v. 5). Consider their subject matter, for example. False teachers find out what people wish to hear and then proceed to proclaim it. Are relativistic sex ethics popular? The false teachers wholeheartedly endorse them. How about the joys of materialism? The teachers are waiting with script in hand.

One way to identify false teachers, then, is to note who hears what they are saying. "The world listens to them," John observes (v. 5). On the flip side of this coin, the world does *not* hear true teaching when it is expounded by genuine teachers: "Whoever is not from God does not listen to us" (v. 6).

Not only do the false teachers choose their subject matter from the world, but they find solutions to man's problems from the world, as well. They propose Band-Aid answers when the victim has gaping spiritual wounds. I spoke with a twenty-five-year-old housewife whose husband was having an affair with one of his co-workers. She had gone to a marriage counselor to ask for help. The counselor said her Christian faith left her with too many inhibitions. He told her to solve her marital problems by having an affair herself! Fortunately, she had enough spiritual discernment not to listen to this advice. She realized this solution came from the world's point of view and would only have compounded her problem.

With so many confusing voices speaking on spiritual issues, how can Christians hope to survive? The answer is, we already have won the victory over false teachers! The Holy Spirit residing in us is greater in power than the spirit of Satan. This fact inspires us with confidence. The Holy Spirit can penetrate the darkness of the human heart. He will "convict the world of guilt in regard to sin and righteousness and judgment" (John 16:8). The Spirit takes the laser beam of the Gospel and convinces sinners of the dangerous condition they are in. This same Spirit can persuade them that Christ is the only remedy. We have overcome the world on both the intellectual and moral level and can appropriate this same overcoming power for others.

The believer who relies on the Holy Spirit, therefore, hears the voice of God in the true teacher. It strikes a responsive chord in him. This is what Jesus meant when He said, "My sheep listen to My voice; I know them, and they follow Me" (John 10:27).

We must hear and respond in obedience. We must constantly monitor the messages we receive. We must ask ourselves, "Am I hearing the voice of God, or the voice of man?"

Making this determination is not always easy. Striving to maintain orthodoxy can be a difficult and confusing process. In advocating orthodoxy, though, John is not suggesting that disagreements must entirely vanish from the church. Nor does 1 John teach that if a brother and I disagree over the interpretation of a single Scripture verse, we should oppose one another.

It is important to note that John uses the collective "we" in 4:6. He is not speaking as an isolated voice, but identifies himself—and us—with the collective truth of apostolic doctrine. In other words, there are certain fundamentals of the faith to which all Christians should give allegiance. Yet we also can allow for individual differences of opinion on nonessentials. In this way, God's family can achieve and maintain the type of love and unity we need to be a vital force in a hostile world.

1 John 4:7-21

⁷Dear friends, let us love one another, for love comes from God. Everyone who loves has been born of God and knows God. ⁸Whoever does not love does not know God, because God is love. ⁹This is how God showed His love among us: He sent His one and only Son into the world that we might live through Him. ¹⁰This is love: not that we loved God, but that He loved us and sent His Son as an atoning sacrifice for our sins. ¹¹Dear friends, since God so loved us, we also ought to love one another. ¹²No one has ever seen God; but if we love each other, God lives in us and His love is made complete in us. ¹³We know that we live in Him and He in us, because He has given us of His Spirit. ¹⁴And we have seen and testify that the Father has sent His Son to be the Saviour of the world. ¹⁵If anyone acknowledges that Jesus is the Son of God, God lives in Him and he in God. ¹⁶And so we know and rely on the love God has for us. God is love. Whoever lives in love lives in God, and God in him. ¹⁷Love is made complete among us so that we will have confidence on the day of judgment, because in this world we are like Him. ¹⁸There is no fear in love. But perfect love drives out fear, because fear has to do with punishment. The man who fears is not made perfect in love. ¹⁹We love because He first loved us. ²⁰If anyone says, "I love God," yet hates his brother, he is a liar. For anyone who does not love his brother, whom he has seen, cannot love God, whom he has not seen. ²¹And He has given us this command: Whoever loves God must also love his brother.

10 You Can't Afford to Be without It

A young farm boy traveled to the county fair early one Saturday morning. He spent the entire day taking in sights and sounds he had never experienced before. He watched the games of chance, and visited the various sideshows. He noted the inflated prices charged for rubber-tasting hamburgers, sticky cotton candy, and a multitude of useless souvenirs.

He came home long after dark, footsore and weary. "What impressed you the most, Son?" his father asked. The boy reviewed the day in his mind. Finally, he replied, "I never saw so many things a person could do without."

This farm boy's honest appraisal of that county fair could apply to life as a whole. Just think of all the things we could easily do without:

> Traffic jams
> Root-canal surgery
> Rude store clerks
> Tasteless TV commercials

A list of things we could cheerfully do without in the *church* would not be far behind:

> Misspelled words in the Sunday bulletin
> Interminable business meetings
> Garish bumper stickers that read,
>   "Honk If You Love Jesus"
> Backbiting gossip

Before we go too far, though, we need to compile another list: a list of things Christians *cannot* afford to be without. If you leaf through your New Testament, you'll find one item near the top of everyone's list. As Paul puts it: "And now these three remain: faith, hope, and love. But the greatest of these is love" (1 Cor. 13:13). Love is one thing believers cannot do without.

The Apostle John gives a hearty amen to that sentiment. He never tires of expounding on the theme of love. He explains it in 1 John 2, describes it in chapter 3, and returns to it here in chapter 4. He wants to make certain we understand what love's all about, so he approaches his favorite subject from yet another angle.

John's analysis of love in 4:7-21 is developed in a twofold way. First, he claims that love has a divine source because God's very nature is love (4:7-12). Then, he notes that love has a human embodiment; that is, it must be perfected in us and displayed through our personality (4:13-21).

Love Has a Divine Source (4:7-12)

Its Divine Origin (vv. 7-8). John affirms two truths, with the second explaining the first. He states, "Love comes from God" (v. 7) and "God is love" (v. 8). As Christians, we sometimes fear we'll never be able to fulfill the love commands of the New Testament. "I don't picture myself as a caring person," we explain.

"I have enough trouble loving my own children, not to mention someone else's," we rationalize.

"If you knew my neighbors, you'd see why love is not high on my list," we apologize.

John wants to take the drudgery out of love for us. If we are children of God, we possess God's life and God's nature. And if God's intrinsic nature is love, we must allow that nature to display itself through our personalities. Just as the rays of the sun filter through stained-glass windows and diffuse their warmth, so God uses our varied personalities to disseminate the warmth of His love and care.

A person with a selfish nature will automatically display that nature in selfish acts. One who has a critical spirit will evidence that tendency by finding fault with those around him. In the same way, a person who possesses God's nature—which is love—will reveal that he is born of God by acts of compassion. Such behavior is not always easy, nor is it automatic. Yet we are not dependent solely on our own resources; we can tap the infinite resources of the God of love within us!

By doing so, we can ensure that the quality of our love will be supernatural. *God* loves because it is His nature. *We* love because we have a need. C.S. Lewis, in his book, *The Four Loves*, astutely observes the difference between "need love" and "gift love." "Need love" is represented by the mother who stifles or smothers her child with affection. She is overly eager to meet her child's needs. Why? Because she has a tremendous need, herself: to succeed as a parent. With God, it is different. "In Him there is not hunger that needs to be filled, only plenteousness that desires to give" (Lewis, *Four Loves,* Harcourt,

Brace, Jovanovich, pp. 144-145). Since we have
God's nature, we can exhibit His "gift love" to the
world.

Its Historic Manifestation (vv. 9-12). God's very
essence is love, but people cannot see *an essence.*
Therefore, He has shown His love historically in
Christ (vv. 9-11) and demonstrated it personally
through us (v. 12).

We now return to a theme that John examined in
1 John 3. There we learned that God clearly demonstrated His love by sending His Son and by giving that
Son in death. The only difference between John's
treatment of love in 3:16-18, and his current analysis
of it, is that in the earlier passage, *Christ* was described as giving His life in love; it is God the *Father*
who gives in love in chapter 4. He sent His one and
only Son to die a sacrificial death so we might have
life. Several additional aspects of God's "gift love"
emerge in verses 9-12.

(1) Love must be demonstrated in a clear fashion.
Some people are extrememly awkward or self-
conscious in their attempts to show their feelings of
concern for others. This probably is because love is
similar to a language that must be learned. If you
learn a language as a child, you usually can speak it
fluently and effortlessly later in life. But if you try to
master a foreign tongue when you're older, it is not
as easily done.

Our twenty-year-old son left this morning for Mex-
ico City where he'll be involved in a short-term
missionary project. For the past few weeks, Steve has
been practicing his Spanish on the rest of the family.
He has difficulty speaking the language naturally; his
speech has a mechanical, textbook flavor to it. Over
the next few months his facility for the language
undoubtedly will increase. But he will never master

it as readily as he would have had he learned it as a child.

Love is like that. Many children never receive love during their growing years and so never learn to express it in a natural, uninhibited way. Expressing and showing concern may be difficult for you. You may feel clumsy in extending yourself warmly to others. You are embarrassed as you try publicly to minister to the needs of others. What can you do? Simply ask God to help you be a good learner. Ask Him to show you how to express love in a clear and natural way.

(2) Love must be demonstrated in a costly fashion. God showed His love, not by offering us something that had no value to Him, but by giving His only Son. Likewise, we must not respond to others with mere token love.

A few days ago, a teenaged boy knocked on my door and explained that he was involved in a project to help disadvantaged youths in a neighboring community. "Would you be willing to make a small contribution?" he inquired. I asked a few questions about the project and read a pamphlet he handed me. I discovered he worked for a worthwhile Christian organization that needed my support. I dug into my wallet and made a small contribution. A few weeks later, I received a receipt for my gift in the mail. I had to think for several minutes before I could remember to whom I had made the contribution. I had given willingly, but my contribution hardly was sacrificial. It did not disrupt my life one bit.

God, however, sent us the very best—His Son. The fact that God did not spare His own Son, but delivered Him up freely on our behalf, indicates there is nothing He will not do for us (Rom. 8:34). *Our* love should mirror this example.

(3) Love must reach the unlovable. God did not wait for us to love Him first. He did not defer His love until He was certain we would reciprocate. "This is love: not that we loved God, but that He loved us" (1 John 4:10).

We sometimes like to pick and choose the people to whom our love will be directed. We want God to send us people who will be worthy of our love. We want people who will genuinely appreciate what we are doing for them. We want to love people who are *easy* to love.

Now contrast this attitude with God's. "You see, at just the right time, when we were still powerless, Christ died for the ungodly. Very rarely will anyone die for a righteous man, though for a good man some might possibly dare to die. But God demonstrates His own love for us in this: While we were still sinners, Christ died for us" (Rom. 5:6-8). What's incredible is there was nothing lovable about us. We were belligerent spiritual rebels. We had shaken our fists at the God who created us. We told Him to stay out of our lives. Yet our rejection of God did not keep Him from sharing His love. His love was no less lavish because it was undeserved.

As members of God's family, we also need to reach out to the unlovable. This may require us to befriend a member of the Christian family who has all the qualities we detest. We may have to respond positively to a neighbor who is difficult and unreasonable. But if God did that for us, should we be striving to do less? How else can we expect the outside world to believe our faith makes a difference if we do not practice the fundamentals ourselves?

Its Personal Demonstration (v. 12). The love God bestowed so freely 2,000 years ago must be accompanied by a personal demonstration that can be observed today. Even though God is love, "No one has ever seen God" (v. 12). The implication is clear. People may not see God—but they do see us. God lives in us and the circuit is not complete until people see a personal demonstration of His love in our lives. When God sent His message of love to us, He did more than mail a tract. He put in a personal appearance through His Son, Jesus Christ. His love was incarnated in a human being, and this Man came to establish contact with the very ones He was sent to help. Our love surely cannot be anything less than that.

We also need to personalize our love. Rather than sending a card, helpful as that may be, we should go to the hospital in person. We should follow up a phone call with a personal visit. We should offer our services to someone who is struggling with a trial.

Ten years ago, I received a phone call informing me that the brother of a woman in our church had taken his own life. His funeral was that very afternoon and I was asked to stop by. I knew this woman in a casual way, but I had never met her brother. Still, I felt that God was directing me to attend the service. When I entered the door of the funeral home, the woman spotted me, left her family, and threw her arms around me. Before I could offer a word of comfort or condolence she cried out, "You came. You came."

Five years later, I met this lady again. "I will never forget what you did," she said. "You came to my brother's funeral." I had preached no eloquent sermon. I had not even offered more than a word or two of comfort. I certainly had not solved the unanswered questions surrounding her brother's death. But I learned an important lesson. Sometimes you do a lot of good just by showing up.

Love Has a Human Embodiment
(4:13-21)

Two statements in verse 12 form the headings for this section: "God lives in us" and "His love is made complete in us." This first statement is explained in verses 13-16, the second in verses 17-21.

These two truths are interrelated in that love must be demonstrated in a contemporary, personal way through our lives; yet this is possible only because God lives in us and gives us the power to carry out the command.

God Lives in Us (vv. 13-16). In three separate verses, John tells us of the relationship which exists between Christ and the believer:

- We live in Him and He in us (v. 13)
- God lives in Him and He in God (v. 15)
- Whoever lives in love, lives in God and God in him (v. 16)

This spiritual union between Christ *and* the believer is essential to a loving relationship *between* believers. We noted earlier that Jesus described this union in John 15:1-4. He said it is like the life which flows through the vine into the branches. In the same way, Christ is in us and we are in Christ.

Paul expresses a similar thought: "I have been crucified with Christ and I no longer live, but Christ lives in me" (Gal. 2:20). It is important to understand what is being taught here. These verses are not saying that I must surrender my identity or my individuality. Sometimes people think a dynamic Christian life involves "all of Christ and none of me." This can be somewhat misleading. It suggests that God turns on His huge copying machine in the sky and we all come out looking the same. Everyone acts and thinks like a group of spiritual clones. This is not what Paul means. Christ is living in me, to be sure, but He has not eliminated the "me!"

I talked last week with a recently married couple. Their relationship is a healthy one and neither partner tries to dominate the other. By becoming one as husband and wife, they haven't surrendered their individuality. Rather, their oneness has *enhanced* their individual personalities. Likewise, a healthy relationship with Christ is the best possible way to unlock that unique potential within us.

Because God lives in us, we can understand why God sent His Son (1 John 4:14) and know that Jesus is the Son of God (v. 15). John then takes these thoughts one step further: "We know and rely on the love God has for us" (v. 16). In other words, I am able to know that He loved me personally and sent His Son to die for me individually. These are facts we can rely on.

His Love Is Made Complete in Us (vv. 17-21). In the second part of v. 12, John explained that God's love is made complete in us because we possess His life. He alludes to this fact again when he states, "Love is made complete among us" (v. 17), and when he refers to "perfect love" (v. 18). By mentioning the concept of perfect or complete love, John is indicating that this love is mature and responds both to God and others in a proper manner.

Joe and Karen tell everyone they are in love. Both are eighteen and find it difficult to spend even a few moments away from one another. They talk about marriage, but neither one holds down a permanent job. Joe, in fact, has never been employed for more than a few months at a time. Karen consistently spends more than she makes. Recently, they told some older married friends they'd like to get married. The older couple expressed some reservations about whether Joe and Karen were ready for such a commitment. Joe disagreed. "We're in love," he argued, "and that's all that matters. Our love for each other will overcome these minor difficulties."

Poor Joe. He does not realize that his and Karen's love has not grown up. Theirs is more a case of infatuation than a mature commitment. If they proceed with this marriage, they are in for some real turbulence. If their love *really* were mature, it would be evidenced in their actions and attitudes.

The same is true with the type of love Christians exhibit. If our love is mature or complete, there will be some obvious proofs of it. John lists these proofs in this passage. A mature love expresses itself in confidence toward God and in concrete acts of caring toward our fellow Christians.

(1) Confidence toward God (vv. 17-18). Christians do not have to fear judgment if our love relationship with God is a mature one. Nor do we need to fear the future, because God is dealing with us constructively in the present. He treats us just as He treated His own Son. John explains this truth by claiming, "In this world we are like Him" (v. 17).

Fourteen years ago, when our family was looking to buy a home, a friend indicated he might be able to help us. "I'd like to introduce you to a Christian man who owns a new housing development," he said. "His homes have an excellent reputation and if he has anything that meets your needs, I know he'd be glad to help you." A few days later, we met the builder and told him the area of town in which we wanted to live.

"That subdivision is completely sold out," he explained, "but there's one house left. The potential buyers couldn't come up with the down payment for it. If it's within your price range, I'd be happy to let you have it."

We toured the house and immediately fell in love with it. The next day, we went by the sales office and explained we were interested in the house. The salesman told us that all the homes in that area were sold. We'd have to purchase one elsewhere. I then explained that we had talked to the owner of the development, and he had offered the home to us. Suddenly we received special treatment. The proper papers were produced, the keys to the home materialized, and we were welcomed to the neighborhood. The message was clear. If you know the owner, you'll receive special treatment.

This is what gives us confidence in our relationship with God. The Father treats us in the same way He treated His Son when He was here in this world. The care, protection, and loving relationship that existed between God and His Son is the type of relationship that exists between God and ourselves.

(2) Concrete love before men (vv. 19-21). Verse 18 reminds us that fear and love are mutually exclusive. This truth is easily observed in human relationships. A wife who loves her husband knows he always acts with her best interest at heart. She is not afraid he will harm her, nor is she hesitant to share her true feelings with him. Because he loves her, she feels free to respond in kind.

John is discussing this same truth in terms of our relationship with God. When we no longer need to fear His wrath, we are able to respond to Him in love. We can love because He first loved us. Our loving response to God was preceded by His loving acceptance of us.

There is an important lesson here. God did not wait to see how we would respond to Him before He decided to love us. Therefore, we should not wait until members of God's family respond to *us* before we love *them*. We sometimes fail to help others because "they don't ask for help." It's as though we're waiting for needy people to acknowledge our existence before we come to their aid. The fact is, some people simply will never ask for help. They are too embarrassed or too proud. But that doesn't change the fact that they *do* need help. God did not wait to be asked before He sent His Son. Likewise, we should not wait for an engraved invitation to minister sacrificially to someone else.

God, then, is not the only One to whom we should respond in love. We also should respond in love to one another. In fact, the test of our love for God is proven by our love for others. Once again, our horizontal relationships are proof of our vertical one. The tangible proves the intangible. We cannot speak in glowing terms of our love for God if we overlook obvious needs on our doorstep. It is sheer hypocrisy for us to claim that we can relate to God in love, yet respond with hatred to our brother.

Many years ago, when I was dating the young lady who is now my wife, we had a misunderstanding and I decided to break off our relationship. I came home late that night feeling very despondent. Helen's picture sat on my desk. As I looked at it, I decided that since the relationship was over, I should dispose of the photograph. I removed it from the frame, tore it into tiny pieces, and threw it in the wastepaper basket. The next morning, my college roommate noticed the picture in the garbage and came to the obvious conclusion. I hadn't said anything to him about the broken relationship, but I didn't really need to. My observable behavior told him about something he had *not* observed. He immediately knew the relationship was in trouble. (Fortunately, a few weeks later, Helen and I were able to resolve our differences and start over again.)

"Look at how a Christian treats a brother or sister," John says. "If all you see are his deteriorating relationships, you'll know that what you can't see (his relationship with God) is in trouble as well."

"Whoever loves God must also love his brother" (v. 21). This is God's command. Jesus told us that we are to love God with our whole being and that we are to love our neighbor as ourselves (Mark 12:29-31). If we try to love God without loving our neighbor, our efforts will degenerate into an unhealthy mysticism. If we endeavor to love our neighbor without loving God, we're practicing an insipid humanitarianism.

We must keep these two commands together. What God has joined together, we in His family must not put asunder.

1 John 5:1-12

[1]Everyone who believes that Jesus is the Christ is born of God, and everyone who loves the father loves His child as well. [2]This is how we know that we love the children of God: by loving God and carrying out His commands. [3]This is love for God: to obey His commands. And His commands are not burdensome, [4]for everyone born of God has overcome the world. This is the victory that has overcome the world, even our faith. [5]Who is it that overcomes the world? Only he who believes that Jesus is the Son of God. [6]This is the one who came by water and blood—Jesus Christ. He did not come by water only, but by water and blood. And it is the Spirit who testifies, because the Spirit is the truth. [7]For there are three that testify: [8]the Spirit, the water, and the blood; and the three are in agreement. [9]We accept man's testimony, but God's testimony is greater because it is the testimony of God, which He has given about His Son. [10]Anyone who believes in the Son of God has this testimony in his heart. Anyone who does not believe God has made Him out to be a liar, because he has not believed the testimony God has given about His Son. [11]And this is the testimony: God has given us eternal life, and this life is in His Son. [12]He who has the Son has life; he who does not have the Son of God does not have life.

11 The Facts
of Life

Picture, as a recent magazine cartoon did, two small children sitting beside a Christmas tree. Mountains of used wrapping paper surround them. Books, dolls, electric trains, and stuffed animals occupy every available inch of the living room floor. After surveying their presents, the children finally gaze up at their parents. With dejection written across their faces, they ask, simply, "Is this all there is?"

In our consumer-oriented society, we are surrounded by home computers, air-conditioned automobiles, and fiberglass sailboats. We sit in our designer jeans, dreaming of last year's Hawaiian vacation as we plan this winter's ski trip to Aspen. Yet in the midst of our relentless pursuit of more, more, more, many of us are finding a vacuum in our lives—a vacuum possessions can't fill. Suddenly, we want to turn to our mate and ask, "Is this all there is? Is this all there is to life?"

God's answer is, no! We can find a full and satisfying life in a relationship with Jesus Christ. That is why He visited this planet and took a human body. That is why He endured death on a cross. As Christ Himself explained: "I have come that they may have life, and have it to the full" (John 10:10).

John wants to introduce us to this life, just as he did in the first two verses of this epistle: "This we proclaim concerning the Word of life. The life appeared; we have seen it and testify to it, and we proclaim to you the eternal life, which was with the Father and has appeared to us" (1 John 1:1-2).

The teaching of 5:1-12 builds on these truths. In fact, this passage tersely sums them up. If we have the Son we have life. If we do not know the Son, we have never really lived (vv. 11-12). This passage also answers two questions for us: first, what are the characteristics of real life? (vv. 1-6) and second, how can we be certain we possess it? (vv. 7-12)

Components of Real Life (5:1-5)

A Miraculous Birth. Our human history began on our birthday. Our earthly mother gave birth to us and our physical lives began. Our spiritual experience also had a beginning. If we belong to the family of God, at some time in the past, God breathed spiritual life into our dead hearts and we were "born of God" (vv. 1, 4).

Jesus explained this fact to a religious heavyweight during a special evening conversation. The religious leader, Nicodemus, had anticipated a pleasant chat about religious issues. But when Jesus said, "You should not be surprised at My saying, 'You must be born again' " (John 3:7), Nicodemus definitely *was* startled. He also was very confused. He had been born once. Wasn't that enough? Jesus patiently explained to Nicodemus that just as his earthly life had a definite beginning, his spiritual life also must have a beginning. He needed to be born of the Spirit.

Nowadays, "born again" language has become common. The growth of evangelical Christianity has caught the interest of TV commentators and national news magazines. This development has been helpful—and harmful—to the cause of biblical Christianity. It's been helpful in that it's made the public more aware of the biblical terminology Jesus Himself used (and which is incorporated in this passage of 1 John).

Yet such terminology also has been misunderstood. Some people have come to view the miraculous birth as a nice "experience," but something that isn't absolutely essential to attain true life. They approach the subject of spiritual birth as though they were considering buying a second car. When people go car shopping, they study the want ads and visit the used-car lots. They do some comparison shopping and try to figure out what a reliable source of transportation is going to cost. After they add in the expense of insurance, gas, and maintenance, they may decide they just can't afford another car. It was a nice thought and it would have made life easier, but the cost was too high.

So too with the new birth. It's a nice idea, and would be helpful in many ways, but many persons decide they can get along fine without it. Jesus teaches differently. This type of birth is an absolute necessity—as the divine "must" of John 3:7 implies.

It's entirely possible you may be reading these words and never have experienced the new birth. I know, I know: Your life isn't falling apart. Your marriage is solid. You aren't an alcoholic. Your job isn't in jeopardy. You think you have no need of Jesus. But if you've never experienced the new birth, you haven't made the choice which determines the difference between real life and death.

Christ came that you might have life and enjoy it abundantly. The gift is yours! Simply confess that you are a sinner (Rom. 3:23), acknowledge that Christ is God's only way of salvation (John 14:6), and invite Him into your life now (John 1:12). If you do so, you'll be able to understand what John means when he speaks of being "born of God" (1 John 5:1).

Mutual Love. John wants to give his favorite theme one parting shot. At the end of chapter 4 he spoke of loving God and loving God's children (vv. 19-21). As we know, these two commands are inseparable components of the real life. Now in chapter 5, the author adds one more twist to this idea. In human terms, if a person loves the father of a household, he'll also love the father's children (v. 1). This should be even more true among members of God's family (v. 2).

We sometimes hear of children who have lost their parents through illness or tragedy. If these children are fortunate, friends of the parents will take responsibility for them. The friends' love for the orphans is based on the love and respect they had for the children's parents.

If this is true in human relationships, it should be even more obvious in spiritual ones. That is, if we love God, we also should love His children—our fellow believers.

Joyful Obedience. Meet Joyce. She is a twenty-year-old, newly married housewife. She considers married life a "job that never ends." Listen as she describes her day: "A sink of dirty dishes is always waiting for me. Mountains of dirty clothes take hours to wade through. The ironing never ends. Bob expects three meals a day. Even though I'm not working outside the home, I feel as though I'm under a tremendous burden. Life was a lot simpler before I was married. This is just too much responsibility for one person to carry."

Now meet Janet, also a newlywed housewife. Janet thrives on married life and is eager to please her husband. Even though she has a full-time nursing job, she finds time to keep the apartment clean and to prepare her husband's favorite dishes. Janet doesn't see her married responsiblities as a drudgery, but a delight.

Why are these two women so different? I suspect their attitude toward household chores reflects the amount of love they feel toward their husbands. Janet uses her responsibilities to demonstrate love to her mate. Joyce, on the other hand, considers every responsibility a heavy burden. This could well mean that the love already has vanished from her marriage.

This illustration can be applied to our love for God. "This is love for God: to obey His commands. And His commands are not burdensome" (v. 3). If our Christian experience gets boring and God's commands seem difficult to obey, we should check up on the quality of our love relationship with Him. Do we feel sluggish and apathetic toward our Christian responsibilities? Is it a chore to read the Bible? Do we omit prayer as part of our daily spiritual routine? Do we witness for Christ out of guilt rather than desire? Do we find it difficult to get out of bed on Sunday morning? Can we recall a time when we were *excited* about these activities?

If we're experiencing problems in these areas, it could be a sign that we have forsaken our first love (Rev. 2:4). We may need to repent and ask God to restore the zeal and commitment we had to Him at the beginning.

A fascinating statement surfaces in the Old Testament story of Jacob and Rachel. Jacob had fallen in love with Rachel; her father, Laban, offered her to Jacob in exchange for seven years of labor. Seven years! Seven years would seem like an eternity to wait for most engaged couples today. Yet we read that "Jacob served seven years to get Rachel, but they seemed like only a few days to him because of his love for her" (Gen. 29:20). Jacob saw the long years of hard work for Rachel as a delight and not a drudgery—because love was the foundation of their relationship.

Non-Christians often look at the Christian faith as a heavy burden to shoulder. They watch Christians going to church and to study groups with their Bibles under their arms. They interpret Christian living as a list of do's and don'ts. *I have enough burdens of my own right now,* they say to themselves. *I don't need another weight to drag me down.* Christians know differently. Christianity isn't only about obeying rules (though that is one vital element). It also involves living out a relationship. Therefore, the more love we have for God in our relationship, the easier we will find it to live in joyful obedience to Him.

Decisive Victory. Some Christians feel burdened and weighed down with responsibilities. Somewhere along the line, the joy of their relationship with God has vanished. One possible reason for this is that they are living lives of defeat when they should be experiencing victory. I just came home from my son's little league baseball game. The last few innings were not a joyous occasion. The final score was 22-6 —in the other team's favor. "It's a lot more fun to play when you're a winner," my son concluded.

Many Christians see themselves as losers—born losers. They cannot get it right in the Christian life.

Despite their good intentions, they stumble and fall each time they determine to move ahead in their Christian experience. They decide it'll always be that way this side of heaven.

God intends for us to be born winners (or more accurately, born-again winners!) This is the promise of 1 John 5:4-5. If we live lives of victory, God's commands will be a joy for us—not a burden. Three times in these verses, we are reminded that we are winners or overcomers:

- Everyone born of God has overcome the world (v. 4)
- This is the victory that has overcome the world (v. 4)
- Who is it that overcomes the world? (v. 5)

In light of these promises, why do we often feel more like the vanquished than the victors? These verses tell us clearly. The difference between winning and losing is faith, or believing that Jesus is the Son of God. The victory is ours because of Calvary. It is up to us to claim that victory by faith on a daily basis.

It is August 1945. In a dense jungle on a South Pacific island, a pocket of Allied soldiers are hiding. Because their radio is broken, they do not know that an armistice has just been signed. The war is over; their side has won. If only they were aware of these developments, they could return to their base and enjoy the fruits of victory.

The decisive battle of the world already has been won at the Cross. But like those soldiers in the jungle, many Christians act as though they haven't heard the war's over. Sin has been defeated. When we lay down our arms, we can come to God in faith and enjoy that victory.

A middle-aged man was sitting on a park bench reading his Bible. His brow was furrowed and his face had a perplexed expression on it. He was trying to understand a difficult passage. A small boy was watching the man and mistook his expression for one of despondency. He hurried up to the gentleman and tapped him on the shoulder. "Don't worry, mister," he said in an encouraging tone, pointing to the open Bible on the man's lap. "I read the last chapter in that book—and we win!"

Jesus Christ and His followers are the ultimate winners. Some day Christ will return in triumph and all people will acknowledge Him as Lord (Phil. 2:9). Even now, however, we can live like overcomers if we walk by faith on a daily basis.

The Assurance of Real Life (5:6-12)

They rang my doorbell early one Saturday morning. The older lady was well into her sixties and looked experienced at this sort of thing. Her younger companion, clutching a briefcase stuffed with literature, obviously was a novice.

They had come to visit me, they explained, to hear my views on the problems facing the world. After a few moments of conversation, I realized these two women were members of a well-known cult. They apparently pictured me as a potential convert.

"Let me ask you a question," I said. "Suppose you both were to die before nightfall. You stand before God and He looks over your record. Do you have any assurance He would let you into heaven?"

They both responded negatively. "It's impossible to know," they chimed in unison. "That would be the height of presumption."

I asked another question. "Do you know if you

possess eternal life?"

Once again, they responded it was impossible to know such a thing. They wanted to know how *anyone* could be sure of eternal life.

I took their Bible and turned to 1 John 5. I read verses 11-13 to them, a passage which states that if we have the Son, we have eternal life—and can *know* it. My visitors were at a loss to explain these verses. They soon were on their way.

You do not have to be a member of a cult to lack certainty about your relationship with God. I have known believers who have professed Christ for years, but then have anxious periods in their lives when they question their faith. Sometimes a teenager raised in a Christian home struggles to make his parents' faith his own. He realizes he cannot live the Christian life by proxy. At other times, older people may experience a crisis of faith due to emotional or financial upheavals.

Whatever the reason, there comes a time in many Christians' lives when they need proof that their faith is genuine. John deals with this vital issue in this section of his first epistle (vv. 6-12). We are sure about our faith, he explains, because we have witnesses to back it up. In a courtroom, a lawyer will search out credible witnesses to support the point he is making. In the spiritual realm, we have three witnesses who will testify on our behalf: "For there are three that testify: the Spirit, the water, and the blood; and the three are in agreement" (v. 7). We must now identify these three witnesses and determine why they are so important to our faith.

The Water and the Blood. The fifth chapter of this epistle tells us that Christ is the One who came by water and blood (v. 6) and that these elements constitute two of the three witnesses to our faith. This is a puzzling statement and has been interpreted in a number of ways. Some commentators feel it refers to baptism and the Lord's Supper. Others see it as a parallel to John 19:34, where Christ hanged on the cross and blood and water gushed from His wounded side. Still others see it as a symbolic statement speaking of cleansing and redemption.

However, the word "came" in verse 6 would seem to suggest a reference to Christ's earthly life and His coming to earth. A plausible explanation of this phrase, then, is that it refers to His baptism in water and His death on the cross. The false teachers of John's day taught that Jesus' divinity came upon Him at His baptism and then left Him at the cross. They denied that Jesus was the God-Man from His birth to His ascension into heaven.

This phrase is significant for us because it indicates that the life and death of Christ—contrary to the false teachers' belief—were real historical events. This is why these two witnesses are so important. If Jesus, the God-Man, did not live and die, our faith has no certainty. But if these events *did* take place, they furnish an objective basis for eternal life. The fact is, the Christian message is not based on fables or fairy tales, as many today would have us believe. Rather, these events, along with the Resurrection, are the most firmly established historical happenings of the first century.

The Spirit as a Witness. The third witness John mentions is the Spirit. The events of Christ's life and death are no different from any other event in history—unless the Holy Spirit reveals their inner meaning to us. Picture yourself as a religious leader in the crowd at Jesus' water baptism. Jesus has just condemned your religious life as a spiritual charade. He has told you that being a member of the Jewish nation does not guarantee you a place in God's kingdom. You see Jesus baptized. Still, you fail to grasp the spiritual significance of all that is taking place before your eyes. Why? Because the Spirit has not revealed its meaning to you.

Suppose you are a casual observer at the Crucifixion. You see Jesus struggling under the weight of the crossbeam as He is marched through the city streets. You follow Him to the place outside the city where guilty criminals are put to death. You see Him hang on the cross, notice the ensuing darkness, and hear the cries from His lips. Yet you will not understand what these events mean—unless the Holy Spirit testifies to their significance.

The same is true today. Almost everyone you meet believes that a historical figure named Jesus existed and that He died on a cross. But they will not understand that Christ died for *them*—unless the Holy Spirit reveals it to them.

Scripture states that "The Spirit Himself testifies with our spirit that we are God's children" (Rom. 8:16). Stu saw an accident one Wednesday night around 8:00. A late model Pontiac went through several red traffic lights before smashing into a young man on a motorcycle. A police officer took down Stu's testimony and he was called as a witness at the subsequent trial. The lawyer defending the car driver tried to find inconsistencies in Stu's story, but Stu insisted that the driver of the car—not the motorcyclist—was at fault. When he came off the witness stand, Stu was beginning to doubt he had seen the accident accurately. But then another witness got up to testify and reaffirmed everything Stu had said. Stu's doubts disappeared with the corroboration of the second witness.

The Holy Spirit performs this same work in our

hearts. He takes the objective facts of the Gospel and testifies to their truth and inner meaning. When doubts arise within us as to the reality of our own Christian experience, the Holy Spirit is there to reassure us. One of Satan's major roles is to unsettle our faith. But once again, greater is the Spirit in us than the one in the world.

The Necessity of Faith (5:9-11)

Everyone has faith in someone or something. We have faith in our dentist when he tells us we need a tooth filled. We believe doctors and pharmacists when they write out and fill prescriptions to alleviate our hay fever or allergies. We normally have faith in the cars we drive and the transportation systems we use. If a bus driver tells me his bus is going downtown, I'm willing to believe him.

The point of verse 9, then, is that we simply cannot say we have no faith. We cannot live in the world for a single day without putting our trust in people and things. Appropriately, John notes that "We accept man's testimony." Yet the witness of men and their information is imperfect at best. We take our umbrellas when the weatherman says it will rain—even though we know he's wrong 50 percent of the time. We buy a new car based on a friend's recommendation—even though we know he's been mistaken about other things.

If we believe fallible men, should we not have more faith in an infallible God? He has never let us down. He has never deceived us. And in what does God want us to believe? The testimony He has given us about His Son (v. 9).

This is a matter of life and death. The more serious an issue is, the more important it is that we pay attention to it. If someone tells me to change my brand of toothpaste, I know the world won't end if I ignore that bit of advice. But if a doctor tells me I need an operation that will save my life, I'm more apt to believe him and respond appropriately.

Some people are hesitant to place their faith in Christ because they have unanswered questions about Him. Christianity has facets they do not understand. They need to make extensive inquiries and have *all* their doubts satisfied before they can accept Jesus as their Saviour.

A little reflection, however, will reveal that we rarely have all the information we need to make major decisions in life. Mark is twenty-five years old and has been dating Sheila for almost two years. He has discovered they share a number of common interests, including horseback riding, country and western music, and Chinese food. He also appreciates her sense of humor and her ability to talk about the serious issues of life. Mark has decided he wants to spend the rest of his life with Sheila and suspects she feels the same way about him. He is ready to make a life commitment. There's still a lot about Sheila he doesn't know, but if he waited until he knew *everything* about her, he'd *never* get married. In essence, he feels that the information he has now is sufficient to make a decision. He is willing to make a commitment on limited—but adequate—evidence.

This same principle applies to faith. You'll never answer *all* your questions about God. You may have doubts and fears about how you will make out as a Christian. But you *can* know enough to make a decision. Through the Bible, God has told us enough about Christ, the Christian life, and what lies ahead in the next life to allow us to make a commitment to Him. Our information is not absolute. But it is sufficient.

To deny God's testimony about His Son is a serious offense. In effect, it amounts to calling God a liar (v. 10) and saying we do not want His Son in our lives. It amounts to rejecting His offer of a real, abundant life that will last forever. As John Stott has cogently observed, "Unbelief is not a misfortune to be pitied, it is a sin to be deplored" (*The Epistles of John,* Tyndale, p. 182).

May we have the faith, then, to believe that God *has* offered us a new life through His Son. And may we have the wisdom to appropriate that life on a daily basis as members of His family.

1 John 5:13-21

¹³I write these things to you who believe in the name of the Son of God so that you may know that you have eternal life. ¹⁴This is the assurance we have in approaching God: that if we ask anything according to His will, He hears us. ¹⁵And if we know that He hears us—whatever we ask—we know we have what we asked of Him. ¹⁶If anyone sees his brother commit a sin that does not lead to death, he should pray and God will give him life. I refer to those whose sin does not lead to death. There is a sin that leads to death. I am not saying that he should pray about that. ¹⁷All wrongdoing is sin, and there is sin that does not lead to death. ¹⁸We know that anyone born of God does not continue to sin; the One who was born of God keeps him safe, and the evil one does not touch him. ¹⁹We know that we are children of God, and that the whole world is under the control of the evil one. ²⁰We know also that the Son of God has come and has given us understanding, so that we may know Him who is true. And we are in Him who is true—even in His Son Jesus Christ. He is the true God and eternal life. ²¹Dear children, keep yourselves from idols.

12 It's Great
to Be Sure

"It's a terrible thing to come to the end of your life and not be sure." My elderly aunt spoke those words to me as she lay in a darkened hospital room. She had been sick for some months, had suffered several strokes, and had come to realize her days on earth were numbered. She also had come to realize she had no assurance of eternal life.

We had talked about spiritual things in the past, but my aunt always claimed such matters did not interest her. Now they did. I took out a New Testament and read several verses to her. They were verses of assurance, verses which taught that Christians can know their ultimate destination *before* they leave this life. To the best of my knowledge, my aunt received Christ as her Lord and Saviour that day; she gained the assurance she so desperately craved. A few weeks later, she died. But she was sure.

In the final verses of 1 John, the Apostle draws together a number of themes that have appeared throughout this epistle. He re-examines prayer, eter-

nal life, Satan, sin, and our place in the family of God.
Interestingly, he uses one all-encompassing concept
to tie these strands together: the knowledge that we
can be certain of our faith. Five times in this closing
section we come across the phrase, "we know." John
attaches these words to his consideration of the
topics mentioned above: eternal life (5:13), answered prayer (5:14-17), and the ability to live
above sin (5:18-21).

Knowledge of Eternal Life (5:13)

This is not the first time John has mentioned the
subject of eternal life in his epistle. Earlier, we read,
"We will have confidence" concerning our future life
(4:17). Yet as we've also seen, false teachers had
stirred up doubts among John's readers. These first-
century Christians weren't entirely sure that eternal
life was theirs. Therefore, John wisely addresses this
theme again.

I sat on a beach last July, watching a small wooden
raft float offshore. Several teenagers were standing on
the raft, while other youths in the water positioned
themselves at its four corners. The swimmers rocked
the raft back and forth, spilling the kids off the slip-
pery wooden surface into the lake. Soaking wet, the
teenagers scrambled back on board and the whole
process started over again.

That scene reminded me of the spiritual turbulence some Christians experience. A variety of forces
agitate the waters of their life, and, at some point,
they feel as though they've been tossed overboard.

Ann has been a Christian for a decade and has
experienced a great deal of growth. However, a poor
self-image has caused her to doubt the reality of her
relationship with God. Last week, for example, she
got into an argument with a neighbor and lost her

temper. Though she later apologized to the neighbor and confessed the incident to God, Ann still felt extremely guilty. *How could God love someone who loses her temper so often?* she wondered. *I must not be a Christian after all.* Obviously, Ann needs the reassuring promise of 1 John 5:13.

George's situation is a little different. He's been taught—incorrectly—that Christians never should experience struggles in their spiritual life. A Bible study teacher reassured George that if God controlled his life, he wouldn't need to worry about his unpaid bills or shaky marriage. Since George still is having problems in these areas, he's concluded something must be seriously wrong with his spirituality. In fact, he's begun to wonder whether he really has eternal life.

Experiences like these are not uncommon. We may become unsettled in our Christian faith for a variety of reasons. John's Gospel was written primarily to bring people into God's family (John 20:30-31); John's first epistle was written to keep them there. This unique letter sought to reach individuals who had taken that initial step of faith, but who now lacked assurance of their salvation.

I should point out, though, that assurance and security are two different things. Picture a miser who mistrusts banks and keeps his life savings in a shoe box. Someone convinces him this is not a wise practice; he should take his money to a bank. The miser finally consents and goes to the local bank, securely clutching his shoe box. Once there, he enters the branch manager's office. In hushed tones, he asks the manager one simple question: Can the bank assure him his money will be safe? The manager takes the miser to the vault and explains that his money will be kept there. It is equipped with a time lock and only the manager knows the combination. Furthermore, the bank has insurance for many millions of dollars, more than enough to cover his deposit. The miser reluctantly relinquishes the contents of the shoe box and opens a new account.

That night, however, he is unable to sleep. He tosses and turns in bed, wondering if his money really is safe. He visualizes an expert team of robbers cutting into the bank vault and making off with his money. Perhaps the manager has deceived him. Perhaps his money isn't insured after all.

The next morning, the miser immediately calls the bank. "Have there been any robberies during the night?" he asks in a panic. He is assured that the vault is intact, his money is safe. The miser breathes a sigh of relief. Actually, his money was secure all along. He simply lacked assurance of that fact. His lack of *assurance,* however, in no way affected the *security* of his wealth.

A Christian may lack assurance of salvation. Yet this doubt cannot affect the security of his spiritual position if he is firmly anchored to the Lord Jesus Christ.

I was leaving home for a weekend conference several months ago, when I discovered my wallet was missing. It contained my driver's license and credit cards, so I went back into the house and started searching for it. The wallet was not to be found. I searched the car; again, I came up empty-handed. The time of my first speaking engagement was drawing close and I could delay no longer. I borrowed some money from my wife and started my trip. For the next hour, I wondered where my wallet could have gone. When I finally arrived at my motel I started unpacking my suitcase and there, under a shirt, was the missing wallet. I hadn't lost it at all.

What I had lost was the assurance that it was in my possession. That lack of assurance had caused me a lot of unnecessary anxiety.

In the spiritual realm, if our relationship with Christ is secure, we cannot lose it. If we have believed in the name of God's Son, we possess eternal life. When I have assurance of those facts, other benefits will follow—benefits John outlines in the following verses.

Assurance of Answered Prayer (5:14-17)

The "sequence of belief" described in this passage is similar to the one we saw in 3:19-22. That is to say, if we are positive about our relationship with God, we will be bold in presenting our requests to Him. An employee who has a good relationship with his immediate superior will feel free to ask him for new office equipment. A believer who is certain of his relationship with God is open and eager to approach his Lord with prayer requests.

This fact raises an obvious question: how can we learn to pray more effectively? Accordingly, John explains ways we can boldly seek God in prayer (vv. 14-15) and illustrates these procedures (vv. 16-17).

An Explanation of the Principles (vv. 14-15). Prayer often is considered a simple procedure. We go to God with our requests and He fills our order from His heavenly treasure chest. Supposedly, this transaction is neither mysterious nor difficult. While there's a measure of truth to this interpretation, prayer is not the "automatic" process some people think it is. A number of conditions must be met if our requests are to be granted.

A few weeks ago, I received an automatic teller card from my bank, along with a brochure that explained the new automatic banking plan. Rather than

164 / Loving God's Family

waiting in long lines to do business with a human teller, I could proceed to a computerized banking machine in the outer lobby of my bank. I simply had to insert my card in the machine to receive the money I needed. I wouldn't have to wait to be served, the brochure assured me. Everything was automatic.

Then I read the brochure more carefully. I began to realize that everything wasn't as simple as it sounded. I had to meet a number of specific conditions before my request could be filled. For example, I had to have an account with the bank. I was not able to draw out more money than was in my account. I had to insert the plastic bank card in the appropriate slot. I had to press the right combination of buttons. I had to enter a special code number known only to me. *Then* I could receive my money—automatically!

Many Christians believe that since God already knows our needs, He will give us whatever we ask—automatically. But teller machines and prayer share at least one thing in common: neither will work if you don't understand how to use them. That is why John includes some "prayer instructions" in this passage of his epistle.

(1) We must state our requests. It would be easy to omit this item, but it needs to be underlined. Why do we need to ask for things, we wonder, if God already knows what we need? (Matt. 6:8) Is it just a formality? Picture a five-year-old child who leaves the table and runs to his room to play with his toys. His parents call him back to the table. "You didn't ask to be excused," they say. The child goes through the motions, asks to be excused, and then is permitted to leave.

We may well wonder if our requests to God aren't

somewhat analogous to that illustration. A little reflec-
tion, however, will indicate that this is not exactly the case. For example, consider the *purpose* of prayer. Prayer is not giving God information that He somehow lacks. It is more an opportunity to fellowship with Him.

When my children were smaller, they often would sit beside me on the sofa when I came home. They would chatter about their stuffed animals and the fact that they were going on a picnic tomorrow. They seldom gave me information I did not already know, but that didn't prevent these little talks from being one of the most enjoyable parts of my day. These weren't times for me to gather information, but to enjoy my children and listen to them talk. Might not the same be true of our prayers to God?

(2) We should ask in the will of God. John tells us that God hears us when we pray in His will (v. 14). It is easy to think of prayer in terms of spiritual arm twisting. Suppose Judy asks her father if she can use the car Saturday afternoon. He tells her she can't, as he'll be using it to drive to his weekly racquetball game. Judy suggests an alternative. She'll call her father's racquetball partner and ask *him* to drive her dad to the game. Judy's father again says no, but this time his denial is not quite as firm. If Judy continues her pleading, she may well bring her father around to her way of thinking. If Judy's father grants her request, it will not really be of his own accord. Rather, Judy will have bent his will to match her own.

When we make requests of God, we must be certain that they are sensitive to His will. Prayer is not wearing God down with a torrent of words and a multitude of reasons why He should comply. It is seeking Him, so that we might better understand the principles of Scripture and become more aware of

His will for our lives. The more open we are to accepting God's will, the more effective our prayers will be.

(3) We must ask in faith. John explains why believers can have faith when they pray. He claims, in essence, that if we ask for something in God's will, we know He hears us. And if we know He hears our request, we also know He will grant it (v. 15). James reinforces this truth in his epistle: "But when he asks, he must believe and not doubt, because he who doubts is like a wave of the sea, blown and tossed by the wind" (James 1:6).

James' passage suggests the inner ambivalence that afflicts the doubting person. Such a person probably will end up with a case of spiritual sea-sickness. His lack of purpose in life is directly related to the lack of faith in his prayers.

An Illustration of the Principles (vv. 16-17). John has established the fact that we must ask in God's will if our prayers are to be effective. He now illustrates this principle in both a positive and negative way.

(1) The positive illustration. A clear example of what it means to pray in the will of God is to pray for a brother who is trapped in sin, to pray that he will experience deliverance. God delights to answer such requests because it is His will that "none should perish" (John 3:16).

The effectiveness of such prayers must not be underestimated. James reminds us of the power that is unleashed through the prayers of a righteous man (James 5:16). He also reminds us: "My brothers, if one of you should wander from the truth and someone should bring him back, remember this: Whoever turns a sinner away from his error will save him from death and cover over a multitude of sins" (James 5:19-20).

John describes the results of praying for an erring person in a similar way: "God will give him life" (1 John 5:16). Since John calls this person a brother, the Apostle obviously is referring to a Christian who already possesses life. Therefore, praying for an erring brother is not a matter of asking God to give him a life he already possesses, but asking Him for that brother's fuller enjoyment of it.

We are not always able to tangibly help an erring brother. His spiritual problems may be larger than anything we can handle. We may not have the maturity needed to give the proper counsel. However, there is one thing we *always* can do, and that is to pray. Such prayers are the clearest illustration John can present to explain what it means to ask for something in God's will.

(2) The negative illustration. Christians often claim that "prayer changes things." But even prayer will not suffice in some situations. If a person sins and that sin "leads to death," no benefit can be derived from praying for such an individual. This puzzling passage has been interpreted in a variety of ways. Since the term "brother" is not repeated in the second part of the verse, many commentators believe John is referring to a non-Christian's sins. This seems logical.

There are times when a person's rejection of the light is so blatant, and his blasphemy of God's Spirit so forceful, that such an individual will never receive Christ. Hell is a place populated with such people, and all the prayer meetings in the world cannot turn these individuals from darkness to light. Their rejection of the light is final; they have asked God to stay out of their life once and for all. In some cases, God may give them exactly what they ask for.

Such situations took place when Jesus was on

earth. Certain religious leaders, for example, rejected the light God gave them. They observed the miracles Jesus performed, yet chose to explain His mighty works in a different way. As a result, Christ accused them of committing an unpardonable sin (Mark 3:24). Their decision was irrevocable. Their destiny was sealed. Prayer no longer could help them.

But how can we know when a person has reached this particular point? In other words, when should we cease praying? I'd suggest it's best to keep praying for someone until God tells you to stop. If you still have a burden to pray for a person, it may be a sign that he or she has not yet reached the proverbial "point of no return."

I remember going to the home of a man a number of years ago to talk with him about his relationship to Christ. His wife had become a Christian that week and he seemed interested as well. He was congenial and open to discussing spiritual things, but it soon became evident that he had no desire to become a Christian. I visited him several times and the result was always the same. For over a year, I prayed for him almost daily. As time went on, though, that prayer burden lifted and I have not prayed for him in about twenty years. I am not suggesting that he committed the sin "leading to death." I am merely saying God sometimes removes the motivation to pray for certain people after a period of time. To persist in prayer in such situations accomplishes nothing.

John concludes this passage by stating, "All wrong-doing is sin" (1 John 5:17). Most sin does not fit the category of sin leading to death, but all of it is serious, nonetheless. We must constantly monitor our lives and confess any known sin, regardless of how insignificant it may seem to us.

The Ability to Conquer Sin (5:18-21)

John's general allusion to sin in verse 17 leads to this final paragraph. Sin is ever-present in the world, but the Christian need not be defeated by it. We have received God's life and with it, the power to overcome our spiritual failures (v. 18a). In addition, we have victory over Satan because of the Cross (vv. 18b-19). A third reason we can overcome sin is that we have discovered reality in Christ (vv. 20-21).

We Have New Life (v. 18a). Two statements in this verse remind us we can have on-going victory in the spiritual battle against Satan. The first is, "Anyone born of God does not continue to sin."

We have discussed statements like this before, particularly in 3:4-9. Like this earlier passage, verse 18 does not teach that Christians will never commit an act of sin. It does mean, however, that old patterns of behavior are broken and our spiritual transformation is continous.

Non-Christians often figure that a Christian's new-found faith is merely a "phase" that will soon pass; they believe the Christian's new birth is simply a fad, a fleeting craze. I once spoke with the parents of a teenager who viewed their son's recent conversion in exactly this way.

"We're worried about Sean," they told me as I visited in their spacious home one Saturday afternoon. "We think it's good to be religious, but Sean's taking it too far. He sits in his room for hours on end and does nothing but read his Bible." They paused for a moment. "But his behavior *has* improved and some of his bad habits *have* disappeared."

Sean's parents went on to explain, however, that they believed he was just passing through a phase. They would be happy when things got back to "normal" again.

I explained to them that Sean's change was *not* a phase—it was due to the new birth. And because his relation with Jesus was real, Sean would not revert to his old way of life. He had been born of God and would not continue to sin as he had before.

The second statement pertaining to spiritual victory in verse 18 is, "The One who was born of God keeps him safe." This reference to the "One born of God" points not to the believer, but to Christ Himself. The one born of God (the believer) is kept safe by the One born of God (Christ). This phrase is a reference to the keeping power of Christ.

Some people think they could never make it as a Christian because they don't have the strength to stay away from sin. To a certain extent, they're right. In our own strength, we're helpless to resist sin. Yet the great truth is, *Christ's* power is there to keep us from sin. As Peter notes, "[We], through faith, are shielded by God's power until the coming of salvation that is ready to be revealed in the last time" (1 Peter 1:5). This truth is an important aspect of our new life.

We Have New Freedom (vv. 18b-19). In this passage, John refers to Satan as the evil one and makes two statements about him: "The evil one does not touch him" (the believer); and "The whole world is under the control of the evil one." The first statement relates to Satan and the believer, while the second refers to Satan and unbelievers.

In both references, it is clear that Satan's power is strong. But in relation to the believer, John claims the evil one's chains have been broken. A cosmic victory was won at the Cross and it is only a matter of time until the devil's influence is completely eliminated. Satan's position is not unlike that of a senator who is defeated in a November election. He may go about performing the same duties for several weeks afterward, but it is only a matter of time until he must leave office. Then he is stripped of his power and the person who defeated him takes over.

This means Satan has no real power over Christians unless we are willing to give it to him. And if we appropriate the well-known prayer, "Lead us not into temptation, but deliver us from the evil one" (Matt. 6:13), Satan cannot snatch us away from God.

Contrast this fact with the other statement made about Satan in verse 19. Most non-Christians simply are not aware of Satan's control over them. Your neighbor certainly doesn't think *he's* under anyone's control. He probably feels he makes his own decisions and determines his own destiny.

Scripture teaches us, however, that the options of the unsaved man actually are limited. He is not free, for example, *not* to sin. He is unable to live a life of righteousness, as defined by God. The power of Satan has bound every area of his personality—his intellect, his emotions, and his will. His chains will fall off only when he finds true spiritual liberty through deliverance in Christ.

We Have a New Perspective (5:20-21)

Because of their relationship with Christ, believers have received the ability to distinguish what is real from what is false. The word "true" appears three times in verse 20; it refers both to God and to His Son, Jesus Christ. Christians often are accused of living in a dream world. Some accuse us of using our faith to escape from the responsiblities of life into a realm of fantasy.

This verse shows us that the opposite is true. It is the non-Christian who seeks to escape reality. He denies the existence of the spiritual world. Even if he *does* acknowledge it, he still runs from the reality of God and His Son.

When a person has found the real thing, he should stay away from the hollow world of make-believe. That is why the final verse of John's first epistle is so appropriate. In verse 21, the Apostle warns us to keep ourselves from idols.

For many years, I could not see the relationship between this verse and the rest of the epistle. It was as though John had a little space left on his parchment and decided to throw in a final warning. The admonition in verse 21, however, comes directly from the truth of verse 20. Verse 20 describes the God who is true, while verse 21 speaks of gods that are false. Paul makes the same point: "You have turned to God from idols to serve the living and true God" (1 Thes. 1:9).

These false gods are not limited to primitive societies. They pervade our high-tech world as well. They are evident in a man's desire to be company president regardless of the cost. They are reflected in the exhilaration some people feel when they have power over others. Let us take the Apostle Paul's warning to heart and not be like those who "worshiped and served created things rather than the Creator—who is forever praised" (Rom. 1:25).

This warning about idolatry is a fitting note on which to close our study of 1 John. We have moved out of the realm of falsehood into the realm of reality. Reality is the key to this epistle's message. If a healthy, growing relationship with Christ is a real part of our lives, His love will be exhibited through our relationships with other Christians. And by holding to this epistle's truths, we can discover the joy of loving God's family.

To my parents,
Denis and Mary Lou Rademacher—
thanks for everything,
especially for not stopping with three

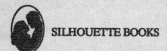

SILHOUETTE BOOKS

ISBN 0-373-19005-0

CHILD OF HER DREAMS

Copyright © 1994 by Sandra E. Steffen

Printed in U.S.A.

CHILD OF
HER DREAMS
Sandra Steffen

Published by Silhouette Books
America's Publisher of Contemporary Romance

Dear Reader,

It's time to celebrate! This month we are thrilled to present our 1000th Silhouette Romance novel—*Regan's Pride*, written by one of your most beloved authors, Diana Palmer. This poignant love story is also the latest addition to her ever-popular LONG TALL TEXANS.

But that's just the start of CELEBRATION 1000! Throughout April, May, June and July we'll be bringing you wonderful romances by authors you've loved for years— Debbie Macomber, Tracy Sinclair and Annette Broadrick. And so many of your new favorites—Suzanne Carey, Laurie Paige, Marie Ferrarella and Elizabeth August.

This month, look for *Marry Me Again* by Suzanne Carey, an intriguing tale of marriage to an irresistible stranger.

The FABULOUS FATHERS continue with *A Father's Promise* by Helen R. Myers. Left to care all alone for his infant son, Big John Paladin sets out to win back the woman he once wronged.

Each month of our celebration we'll also present an author who is brand-new to Silhouette Romance. In April, Sandra Steffen debuts with an enchanting story, *Child of Her Dreams*.

Be sure to look for *The Bachelor Cure*, a delightful love story from the popular Pepper Adams. And don't miss the madcap romantic reunion in *Romancing Cody* by Rena McKay.

We've planned CELEBRATION 1000! for you, our wonderful readers. So, stake out your favorite easy chair and put a Do Not Disturb sign on the door. And get ready to fall in love all over again with Silhouette Romance.

Happy reading!

Anne Canadeo
Senior Editor
Silhouette Romance

Please address questions and book requests to:
Reader Service
U.S.: P.O. Box 1325, Buffalo, NY 14269
Canadian: P.O. Box 1050, Niagara Falls, Ont. L2E 7G7